CONQUER YOUR DEBT

How to Solve Your Credit Problems

WILLIAM KENT BRUNETTE

PRENTICE
HALL
PRESS

New York   London   Toronto   Sydney   Tokyo   Singapore

Disclaimer

This book is intended for information purposes only, and does not purport to offer professional or legal advice on any of the topics discussed. For such advice, you should consult an attorney, accountant, or other professional.

Prentice Hall Press
15 Columbus Circle
New York, NY 10023

Copyright © 1990 by William Kent Brunette

PRENTICE HALL PRESS and colophon are registered trademarks of Simon & Schuster, Inc.

Library of Congress Cataloging-in-Publication Data

Brunette, William Kent.
Conquer your debt: how to solve your credit problems / William Kent Brunette. — 1st Prentice Hall Press ed.
        p.   cm.
ISBN 0-13-172727-3
1. Consumer credit—United States.   I. Title.
HG3756.U54B78   1990
332.024′02—dc20
89-27181
CIP

Designed by Irving Perkins Associates

Manufactured in the United States of America

1   3   5   7   9   10   8   6   4   2

First Edition

This book is dedicated to my parents,
Lois Evelyn (Bush) Brunette and William Jacob Brunette,
who tried to teach financial responsibility to a kid
who simply refused to listen. Some people insist
on learning things the hard way.

Contents

Foreword

Like it or not, we live in a credit economy. This is true whether you're buying a house or a car, taking a vacation, or eating out. If you're a typical American, you're using credit. And you're using it as no people ever have before, anywhere. Household debt, like our federal government's debt and American business debt, is smashing all records. So are family bankruptcies. Our debt is growing much faster than our earnings or our savings.

Managing this colossal credit has become a prime challenge for tens of millions of Americans. *Conquer Your Debt* by Kent Brunette has come along in the nick of time to help bring this exploding problem under control. Here's a book that tells you how to get the most out of your credit. Every American family that reads this book can save thousands of dollars by following its advice.

In recent years Congress has enacted a series of consumer credit laws expressly designed to let us know how to borrow at the lowest cost. Kent Brunette tells you how to take full advantage of those laws. If you have suffered credit discrimination because you are a woman or a member of a minority, or if you have been the victim of untrue charges made to a credit bureau about your credit record, *Conquer Your Debt* tells you how to rectify the situation easily and quickly.

Many Americans have become credit junkies, are married to credit junkies, or have children or parents who have fallen deeply into debt. This book tells you what you can do to help yourself and your loved ones. We sometimes don't recognize how we have become victims of too much borrowing. This book tells you the signals to look for. There's also a remarkable chapter on the basics of conquering your debt.

If you, a member of your family, or a friend have gotten into legal difficulties with your debt, this book gives you expert advice that might cost you an arm and a leg if you had to hire a lawyer to protect you.

This book tells you how to take advantage of a new tax-law provision concerning home equity loans (the one remaining way to deduct interest expenses from your income tax). Here's another way this book will save you a bundle. The book wisely counsels caution in taking out a home equity loan. It gives you guidelines for using this form of borrowing to pay off your other debts. It even suggests when you should check with an adviser.

What I like about this book is that it gives you thoughtful, expert advice on how to use credit. However, it doesn't entice you to borrow more and more. In fact, if you follow the advice in this book, you will slash your interest costs even if you don't reduce your debt. You can also find ways to reduce your credit burden by diminishing the amount you borrow.

Above all, this book is a much-needed antidote to the advertising that swamps us wherever we turn. On television, on our car radio, in our newspapers and magazines, we are constantly besieged to buy, buy, buy—to buy now and pay later. There has never been a time or place when the seduction of immediate consumption has been more compelling. When it comes to borrowing and spending, we need every voice of caution and prudence we can get. Kent Brunette has provided a wonderfully bountiful helping of exactly those in *Conquer Your Debt*.

Should our country suffer another recession, millions of homeowners would lose their jobs. Many of these people would lose their cars and their homes because they couldn't pay their debts. You and your family could be among them. *Conquer Your Debt* could save you from such a disaster.

Even if you are superconservative in your financial behavior, borrow rarely, or borrow well within your ability both to repay and to handle the interest charges, this book will save you a tidy sum.

There's even icing on this cake. *Conquer Your Debt* is a breeze to read. There's no legal gobbledygook. It takes you by the hand and leads you to the land of lower cost and a lot more for your money.

—William Proxmire
United States Senator (retired)
who fathered the consumer credit
statutes during the 1970s

Preface

Most people are exposed to the notion of financial responsibility at an early age. Many of us were forced to live on an allowance, even though we probably finagled far more resources than we were intended to have. "Lunch money" helped us learn how to set spending priorities, often against our better judgment. Most of us remember the day our parents helped us open a savings account. How we marveled at the rate our pennies were growing; how tempted we were to spend our savings at every "important" opportunity!

Regrettably, as we grew up, many of us developed more permissive attitudes toward spending and credit activities. The ready availability of credit allowed us to succumb to a "buy now, pay later" philosophy. While our parents may have limited their use of credit to big-ticket items, like the purchase of a car or refrigerator, many of us came to rely on credit to meet ordinary, day-to-day expenses. Whether it was keeping up with the Joneses or just making do, we ignored the fact that we were borrowing money to perpetuate our life-styles.

Several years ago I suddenly realized that I was overextended and if I did not take some major action, I was well on my way to financial ruin. To resolve my problems, I was forced to change my spending habits and my attitudes toward credit. I contacted my creditors, developed repayment plans, and paid my debts over a couple of years. I became familiar with the contents of my various credit reports and took steps to assure their accuracy and completeness. With my credit problems now behind me, I am cautious with credit and have gained a healthier respect for its proper use.

When I was grappling with my credit problems, I was astonished that there was no single resource that addressed the range of debt and credit issues confronting me. While a great deal of information on financial planning exists, virtually all of it presupposes the existence of financial resources. Since most financial planning materials are geared toward investing for the future, they offered little help in resolving my more immediate credit problems. In addition, I had little access to affordable professional services to help me deal with basic financial-responsibility matters.

Conquer Your Debt was written to fill a significant information void confronting the U.S. debtor population. The book's goal is to help smooth the way for others who are confronting the same (or similar) problems I did. It offers pointers and helpful hints for addressing all your credit needs. *Conquer Your Debt* was written so that you might benefit from the experience of someone who has been there.

Introduction

Consumer Credit Crunch

Personal debt is one of the most pressing problems of American society. Today an estimated 40 million Americans either have problems with credit or have no credit at all.

The current consumer credit crunch is illustrated by the following facts:

"Plastic prosperity" has made credit more readily available than ever before. In 1987, more than 93 million American families held more than 625 million credit cards. The average American family has six different credit cards, and many have more. Only two out of every five of these credit-card-holding families pay their credit card balances in full every month; 60 percent carry credit card debt over from month to month.

Credit card use will continue to increase. Credit applications are everywhere; some come preapproved in the mailbox. Creditors advertise aggressively for credit card business.

Consumer debt is at an all-time high. In January 1979, Americans had a little more than $265 billion in outstanding consumer debt. In the past 10 years, this figure has climbed rapidly, totaling more than $674 billion in January 1989. Consumer indebtedness is expected to continue to climb in the future.

Personal bankruptcies are at an all-time high. Bankruptcy filings increased significantly after federal bankruptcy laws were revised in 1979, and they have skyrocketed in recent years. In 1988, a whopping 613,616 people filed bankruptcy—a tremendous increase over the 473,000 bankruptcies declared in 1987. The number of personal bankruptcies is expected to continue to escalate in the coming years.

What Consumers Don't Know *Is* Hurting Them

Most people do not know how much they do not know about their own financial well-being. This is true for a number of reasons:

- Most people are unaware of the tremendous variety of financial service products on the market today.
- Many people are intimidated by the complexities of financial decisions; thus, rather than shop around and reevaluate these decisions, they prefer to stay with what they have, ignoring available options.
- Great numbers of people are unaware, and not reaping the maximum benefits, of the consumer credit laws designed to protect them.
- Very few people experiencing financial difficulty are taking the required steps to protect themselves as they repay their financial obligations.

Consumers are constantly missing important opportunities to enhance their financial situation. Thus, millions of Americans are undergoing a personal debt crisis.

Conquer Your Debt is a handy resource containing essential, basic information on financial-responsibility issues. It will help you sort through the complexities of financial and credit issues and the legal jargon of the federal consumer statutes. Substantial attention is also given to behavior-modification techniques intended to change attitudes toward credit and spending practices.

The book is full of ideas that can easily be applied to your particular situation. Practical, step-by-step advice will guide you through all your financial and credit-related difficulties. Start at the beginning and follow the topics as they are presented. Each step you take is another step forward in regaining a firm financial footing.

Good luck!

CONQUER
YOUR DEBT

CHAPTER 1

Getting Credit

What Is Credit?

What do you think about when you hear the word *credit*? Do you automatically picture a credit card? Although credit cards may be one of the most popular credit tools available, many different types of credit are used daily. Personal loans, mortgages, store charge accounts, lines of credit, and so on, help millions of Americans accomplish their goals—to pay for their children's educations, buy a home or car, take a vacation, redecorate their homes, or finance medical expenses.

Credit lets us "buy now, pay later." Credit grants us immediate access to services and merchandise. It allows us to enjoy our purchases as we pay for them. It also enables us to purchase big-ticket, expensive items that we would normally have difficulty paying for. For example, rather than having to save for years to accumulate enough money to purchase a new car, we use credit, which allows us to finance the car over a period of years at manageable payment levels.

Credit has also become indispensable to our day-to-day functioning. Without credit it is difficult if not impossible to rent a car, make hotel reservations, or book an airline ticket.

Credit cards have become necessary identification for many daily activities, like cashing a check. Thus, we all need access to credit.

Types of Credit

Since so many types of credit are available today, you should become generally familiar with the various ones you might encounter. Then you can plan your future credit use around the type that most closely fits your needs.

Credit Cards

Have you ever wondered why some of your credit cards are governed either by where you live or where the card was issued? This is because different rules apply to the three different types of credit cards on the market today—bank cards, retail cards, and travel and entertainment cards.

Bank Cards. Bank cards are offered through a bank or financial institution. Bank cards, like VISA, MasterCard, and Discover, represent extensions of credit that allow you to purchase services and items from third parties—someone other than the firm extending credit to you. Bank cards, which allow consumers to pay the monthly balance either in full or in installments, usually require the payment of an annual fee.

If you have a bank card, your credit card agreement is bound by the laws of the state where your bank card company's operations are actually located. For example, if you live in Texas and have a credit card issued by a bank in Delaware, your agreement is subject to Delaware's laws, not those of Texas. Thus, since Delaware law allows a creditor to charge a higher interest rate than is allowed under Texas law, your Delaware bank card may carry the maximum interest rate allowed by Delaware law.

Retail Cards. Retail cards—such as department store, gasoline, and airline charge cards—are credit devices designed to finance purchases you make directly from the company providing the credit. For example, you purchase an item from Sears and use your Sears charge card to finance the transaction. Retail cards, which allow you to pay in full or in installments, normally do not charge an annual fee.

Retail charge card agreements are controlled by the state in which you live. For example, even though Sears may be based in Chicago, if you live in California, it is California law that will govern your Sears charge card. This is why the monthly statements of most retail charge cards usually contain a chart listing the states, along with their applicable interest rates.

Travel and Entertainment Cards. Travel and entertainment cards—such as American Express, Diners Club, and Carte Blanche—are yet another type of credit card. They provide credit availability for third-party purchases. These cards, which require an annual fee, also usually require payment in full of the monthly balance due. If interest is charged or penalties assessed, they are governed by the law of the state in which the customer resides.

Other Frequently Used Types of Credit

Open-End Credit Plans (also known as charge or revolving-credit accounts). These plans allow you repeated transactions on the same account, up to your credit limit. Such plans allow you to pay the balance in full or in installments; finance charges are assessed on the unpaid balance. Minimum payments are normally based on a set percentage of the outstanding balance. Examples include credit cards, lines of credit (for example, overdraft protection on a bank account), and store charge accounts.

Closed-End Credit Plans (also known as installment loans). Such obligations require a set number of equal monthly installments to pay off a predetermined loan amount. Interest is assessed from the date the loan is received. Closed-end plans are often used to finance the purchase of a particular item, which serves as collateral for the loan. Examples include car and personal loans.

Mortgages. A type of closed-end credit plan, with a dwelling as collateral.

Home Equity Loans. Home equity loans allow you to borrow money based on the equity you have amassed in your home. Many such loans are open-ended, since they are for a predetermined limit, which you can either use or have available for your use. (See "Home Equity Loan" section in chapter 8.)

Secured Loans. Such loans require collateral (security) to support the loan. The creditor retains a security interest in the object pledged, which will be forfeited in the event of default.

Unsecured Personal Loans. Unsecured personal loans do not require the use of collateral to support the loan; they are based primarily on your income and your ability to repay.

Debit and Secured Credit Cards

You should also be aware of the existence of debit and secured credit cards. On the surface, you usually can't tell the difference between these and regular bank cards. But the difference is that you don't borrow money from a creditor when you use these cards; you borrow money against funds *you* have on deposit with a creditor.

Debit Cards.   With debit cards, your transactions are automatically debited from a savings, or money market account you maintain with the institution that issued the card. The financial institution never lends you money; it simply allows you to access funds in your account via a debit card. Thus, while transaction fees may be assessed, you don't pay interest charges because you are borrowing from yourself.

Secured Credit Cards.   Secured credit cards allow you to obtain a credit card through the establishment of an account that serves as security for your purchases on the card. For example, if you have a secured credit card that allows you to charge up to $500, you would also be required to maintain an account balance of at least $500 on deposit with the creditor which issued the secured credit card. In the event of your default, the creditor can use your collateral—your $500 on deposit—to cover the purchases you made on the card. Since some creditors tout secured credit cards to people who cannot get credit because of bad credit records or over-extensions, such cards are sometimes fairly expensive, with application fees and transaction charges. For a current listing of the best secured credit cards available, contact:

Bankcard Holders of America
460 Spring Park Place, Suite 1000
Herndon, VA 22070

Access to Credit-Pricing Information

If you are considering applying for credit, you must determine your cost of borrowing, compare these costs, and shop around for credit. All these activities require that you be granted access to crucial credit-pricing information so you can make meaningful credit-purchase decisions. In addition, such activities may require some effort on your part. However, since the cost of credit varies widely, you can really save yourself a lot of money if you simply take the time to carefully evaluate credit decisions before you make them.

The federal Truth-In-Lending Act requires creditors to provide you with access to basic information concerning the costs of credit use. Through the disclosure of such factors as the finance charge, amount financed, and annual percentage rate, you are given crucial pricing information in an easily understandable common language. If you are applying for open-end credit (credit card, department store charge card, or line of credit), your potential creditors must also disclose to you their method of calculating finance charges, and inform you as to when finance charges will accrue on your account. You are entitled to these up-front disclosures *in writing, before* you sign any credit agreements.

The Truth-In-Lending Act also requires the accurate advertising of credit products by creditors. Generally, if a creditor advertises certain credit-pricing components, other important terms of the offering must also be disclosed in the same advertisement.

In addition to the disclosures required by the Truth-In-Lending Act, some states have passed laws that provide additional, complementary protections. The states are free to enact laws providing protections in areas not covered by the Truth-In-Lending Act, so long as the state laws are not incompatible with federal law.

Typical Loan Payments

Before taking out a new loan, you must make absolutely certain you can afford it. The following chart should give you a ballpark estimate of payments for various interest rates, time periods, and amounts.

Simply find the applicable interest rate, look across at the monthly payments required for the various time periods, and multiply by the multiple of 1,000 that represents the total amount of your loan. For example, a $10,000 loan at 14 percent interest would yield approximate monthly payments of either $480.20 ($48.02 × 10) for 24 months, or $341.80 ($34.18 × 10) for 36 months.

MONTHLY PAYMENTS NECESSARY TO AMORTIZE A $1,000 LOAN

Interest Rate (%)	12 Months	24 Months	36 Months	48 Months	60 Months
0	$83.33	$41.67	$27.78	$20.83	$16.67
1	$83.79	$42.12	$28.23	$21.28	$17.12
2	$84.25	$42.57	$28.68	$21.73	$17.57
3	$84.71	$43.02	$29.13	$22.18	$18.03
4	$85.17	$43.47	$29.58	$22.63	$18.49
5	$85.63	$43.92	$30.03	$23.08	$18.95
6	$86.09	$44.37	$30.48	$23.54	$19.41
7	$86.55	$44.82	$30.93	$24.00	$19.87
8	$87.01	$45.27	$31.38	$24.46	$20.33
9	$87.47	$45.72	$31.83	$24.92	$20.79
10	$87.92	$46.15	$32.27	$25.37	$21.25

MONTHLY PAYMENTS NECESSARY TO AMORTIZE A $1,000 LOAN
(*continued*)

Interest Rate (%)	12 Months	24 Months	36 Months	48 Months	60 Months
11	$88.39	$46.61	$32.74	$25.85	$21.75
12	$88.85	$47.08	$33.22	$26.34	$22.25
13	$89.32	$47.55	$33.70	$26.83	$22.76
14	$89.79	$48.02	$34.18	$27.33	$23.27
15	$90.26	$48.49	$34.67	$27.84	$23.79
16	$90.74	$48.97	$35.16	$28.35	$24.32
17	$91.21	$49.45	$35.66	$28.86	$24.86
18	$91.68	$49.93	$36.16	$29.38	$25.40
19	$92.15	$50.41	$36.66	$29.90	$25.94
20	$92.62	$50.89	$37.16	$30.42	$26.48
21	$93.09	$51.37	$37.66	$30.92	$27.02

After you have determined your approximate monthly payments, you should compute your ultimate cost of credit. Using the example above, monthly payments of $480.20 for 24 months yield a total cost of $11,524.80; payments of $341.18 per month for 36 months yield a total cost of $12,282.48. Interest charges based on this $10,000 loan would be $1,524.80 for the 24-month loan; $2,282.48 for the 36-month loan. Thus, one year results in a $757.68 difference in interest charges.

This example graphically illustrates the cost of credit. If you can manage a shorter repayment period, you can save a lot of money. The longer you stretch out your payments, the more you will ultimately pay. Similarly, lower interest rates and lower loan amounts will yield lower ultimate costs.

Shopping for Credit Cards

Think about one of your credit cards. Do you know:

- What interest rate you are paying?
- How much the annual fee is?
- If your card has a grace period (a period during which you may pay your current month's charges without having to pay interest)?

Did you realize that some credit cards:

- Have interest rates as low as 12.5 percent?
- Don't charge an annual fee?
- Offer a twenty-five to thirty-day grace period?

Most people simply do not shop around for credit as they do when buying a car, major appliance, or clothing. Yet credit purchase decisions, particularly credit card transactions, have a tremendous impact upon our day-to-day lives.

Almost half of American credit card holders charge items at least once a week; some people make several charges a day. Since credit card use is an ongoing activity, your card's pricing components are applied to every purchase you make with the card. Thus, the cost of a purchase might increase because a credit card is used for payment.

With the staggering number of financial products on the market today, it is well worth your while to take a hard look at *all* your credit agreements and to compare them with other, currently available products. Also, since new financial products are emerging daily, you should periodically re-evaluate your credit purchase decisions so you can take advantage of the latest offerings. If you are applying for your first credit card, familiarize yourself with each card's features and select the one that best fits your particular needs and spending patterns.

As you begin evaluating different products, you will probably quickly discover there are trade-offs to be made. For example, you may find a card with no or a low annual fee, but it may come with strings attached, like no grace period or a high interest rate. So, evaluate each product carefully. Your best bet will probably be a "balanced" card, one with no gimmicks and moderately priced individual components. Consider the following when evaluating credit card products:

• Maximize your benefit in today's highly competitive credit card market. Shop around—get price information from several financial institutions, listen to television and radio commercials, look in the newspaper, open some of those credit card solicitations that probably come to you in the mail, ask friends which credit cards they have, and so on.

• Find a card that meets your specific needs and spending patterns.

• Consider getting your card from a nonlocal provider (that is, an out-of-state bank) if its offer is superior to what you can obtain locally.

• Be aware that annual fees vary widely—ranging from fifteen to thirty-five dollars for regular cards; fifty dollars and more for premium cards.

• If you normally pay your bill in full each month, make sure to get a card with a grace period. If your card does not have a grace period, finance charges will be assessed from the date you make a purchase or the date a transaction is posted to your account. If your card has a grace period, your creditor must bill you at least fourteen days before your payment is due. This should allow you to make your payments by the due date so you can avoid interest charges.

• If you do not pay your credit card balance in full every month, and wind up paying in installments, find a card with a low interest rate. Similarly, if you use your credit card as a substitute for a personal loan (that is, if you carry a sizable balance due on your card most of the time), the interest rate assumes increased significance.

• Be aware that some credit cards include other types of charges: monthly fees (whether you use the card or not), a transaction fee each time the card is used or when it is used on special transactions (like a cash advance), late payment fees, or over-the-limit penalties.

• Be aware of factors other than cost that should be calculated into your selection decision. These include line-of-credit amount, how widely the card is accepted, purchase protection, travelers' and buyers' assurance programs, credit card registration services, personal check cashing, access to money machine networks, and travelers' checks dispensers, rebate programs, bonus mileage credit under frequent-flyer programs, insurance protection, year-end activities summaries, and other services and features.

To enable you to make more-informed credit card purchase decisions, credit and charge card applications must disclose:

• Interest rate
• Annual fee
• Grace period
• Balance-computation method

Creditors are also required to disclose cash advance fees, late payment fees, and over-the-limit fees associated with their cards. They must also provide accurate information in their credit card advertising, along with key pricing components (if they are included in the advertisement).

To receive listings of financial institutions offering low interest rates or no-annual-fee credit cards contact:

Bankcard Holders of America
460 Spring Park Place, Suite 1000
Herndon, VA 22070

With such pricing information readily available, there is really no excuse not to shop around for the best possible credit card deal. In addition, are you carrying a sizable amount of debt on your credit cards? If your answer is yes, have you shopped around for a personal loan? If you can get a loan at a lower interest rate than you are paying on your credit cards, wouldn't this reduce your ultimate interest costs?

How Do Creditors Make Decisions?

Once a creditor has your credit application in hand, it is "scored" to determine if you will be a good credit risk and whether you will be extended credit.

Just as a teacher may be looking for particular responses when grading a test, creditors also look for specific items they have determined as their credit-scoring criteria. Traditionally, creditors have relied on the "three Cs":

Character—Will You Repay the Debt? Character indicates your willingness to pay, including an evaluation of your stability (length of residence, employment, whether you rent or own) and your credit experiences (amounts you currently owe, whether you pay your bills on time, your credit history).

Capacity—Can You Repay the Debt? Capacity indicates your ability to pay, through an assessment of employment information (what you do for a living and how much you earn) and your expenses (monthly expenses and the number of dependents you have).

Collateral—Is the Creditor Protected? Collateral indicates your available resources, should you fail to repay. Thus, collateral is assets (savings, property, or investments) on which to rely to make good on your obligation. In some cases, creditors will require you to pledge the item obtained on credit (for example, a new car) as collateral for the loan.

Recently, many creditors have merged the "three Cs" into elaborate, computerized credit-scoring systems designed to enable them to predict your repayment performance on prospective extensions of credit. In most credit-scoring systems, creditors will assign different values to such things as your past credit activities, how much money you currently owe other creditors, your income, whether you own a home, how long you've lived at your current residence, if you are employed, how long you've been in your current position, and so on. Creditors will rate you—give you different grades—on the various components of their credit-scoring system. You could be graded on as few as six or as many as fifteen or twenty different factors. Then the creditors will add up your scores. If your total exceeds their cutoff threshold—their passing score—the creditors will probably extend you credit. However, if your total falls short of their threshold, you will probably fail their test and your application will be rejected.

It is possible for one creditor to accept and another to deny your application based on identical information. This is because no single credit-scoring system is used by all creditors. Each creditor develops his own credit-scoring system, based on his own experiences with lending money. He is free to use whichever factors he chooses. So long as he does not illegally discriminate against you on the basis of race, sex, marital status, national origin, religion, or age, creditors are under no obligation to reveal their credit-granting criteria. Such credit-granting criteria are very closely guarded secrets. In addition, creditors are not required to reveal your precise score under their system.

Credit Application Pointers

Keep the following points in mind when applying for credit:

Learn Your Creditor's Criteria.   A financial institution may require you to have a savings account, to maintain a minimum balance on deposit, or to have been a bank customer for a set period of time before you can qualify for certain credit products. Also, since some types of credit are specifically geared toward higher-income people, you might have to meet minimum income standards, have certain spending patterns, and so on, to qualify for specific products.

Before you apply for credit, find out what requirements your creditor may have for the type of credit you desire. If you discover you cannot meet their credit standards, you can save yourself the trouble of applying for the loan. Or, if you know the selection standards before applying for the loan, you can take the necessary steps to assure you meet the criteria. Such inquiries will also help you to shop around for the credit product that meets your precise needs.

Be Aware of Credit Overextension Thresholds.   When deciding if they will extend you additional credit, most creditors place primary importance on your current level of indebtedness. Many will not grant credit if the amount of the new credit and your outstanding credit together will exceed 15 percent of your annual take-home pay. Very few will extend credit if your total indebtedness will be 20 percent of your annual take-home pay or greater.

If you are applying for credit or planning to in the future, you should contact the prospective creditor to ask what are considered to be tolerable credit limits. If your debts exceed these, do not apply for the loan since your application will probably be denied. Why go through the inconvenience of filling out an application form, possibly paying an application fee, and having a creditor inquiry recorded on your credit report if you know your application will be rejected? You may simply have to bring your total indebtedness below a certain level before the loan will be approved, or find another creditor.

Make an Effective Presentation. To assure that the creditor can read the information you provide, it is probably best to type your responses on the credit application. If this is not possible, print legibly. Give all the information requested. If you do not know some of the answers, such as the number on a former account, go through your files or call your former creditor to get the information. If you are having trouble responding to the questions in the spaces provided on the application, add an attachment. Be sure to place a notation in the appropriate space on the application so the creditor will refer to the attachment for that item. Do not skip any items. Because an incomplete application may yield a rejection, be sure to provide all the information requested so your application can be evaluated on its merits.

Put Your Best Foot Forward on the Application. Make sure your responses are presented in their most favorable light. Consider the following suggestions:

Assets. List all assets that you either hold individually or with someone else. Thus, if you and your spouse own a house together or have a joint savings account, list them on the application. Do not include the original value of these assets. Rather, estimate their current value, since these may well have increased since you acquired them. If the house you paid $50,000 for has a current market value of $125,000, list the latter figure. Indicate the estimated current balance in your savings account.

Income.   List your gross income (before any deductions), unless you are specifically requested to indicate the amount of your take-home pay (net income). Make sure your income is stated in the increment requested (annual, monthly, or weekly). If you receive pension or government benefits, list the amounts you receive.

Credit Obligations.   You should make certain to include a listing of your credit obligations on the application. You cannot selectively list your favorable accounts and fail to mention any unfavorable obligations you might have. However, list your best credit accounts first on the application, making certain to include both individual and joint accounts. If you were an authorized user on an account, list the account along with your authorized-user status.

Estimate the current balances due for each of your obligations, rather than the original amount of credit extended. Thus, if you took out a $15,000 car loan three years ago and have one year left on the loan, indicate today's balance rather than the original amount.

If you have unfavorable credit accounts (those you did not pay in a timely fashion, which appear as adverse entries on your credit report), you must include them on your application. However, if these do not accurately reflect your creditworthiness, you should explain this to your potential creditor. For example, suppose you got behind in your bills during a period of unemployment. Now you have a stable job and make twice what you made in your old position. If your creditor knows this, the negative accounts can be viewed in light of the extenuating circumstances.

Additional Information. Since some of your positive credit obligations will be unlikely to appear on your credit report, make certain to affirmatively disclose such information on your application. Once you know which obligations are excluded from your credit report, prepare an attachment, for use with any future credit applications, which lists these favorable obligations. For example, if you have or have had a mortgage, list it on the application, since mortgages are often not reflected on credit reports. This will assure that your potential creditor has a complete credit picture when determining the fate of your application.

You might also offer to help potential creditors verify credit references if an account does not appear on your credit report. Or you might provide creditors with additional information not specifically requested in the application, such as former names or past addresses, so your complete credit history can be accessed.

Keep a Copy of All Applications You Submit. You will probably need to refer to the original application information should you need to follow up with the creditor or pursue an appeal. Also, since your application will be likely to include valuable information about your credit condition (account numbers, balances, and so on), keep it for general reference. Then, if you apply for another loan, you will have the information at your fingertips.

How Creditors Must Respond to Your Application

When you apply for credit, you are entitled to the following rights under the federal Equal Credit Opportunity Act. Your prospective creditor must act on your application within thirty days. If your application is rejected or the loan is approved for a reduced amount, the creditor must either advise you of the reasons for the decision or inform you that you are entitled to know the specific reasons for the declination. If the original rejection letter does not give you the reasons for the adverse action, you may request this information in writing within sixty days. The creditor then has thirty days to respond to your request.

The creditor must cite specific reasons for any adverse action. Permissible reasons for rejecting your credit application may include one of the responses in the sample rejection letter below:

Dear _____:

We regret to inform you that your recent request for an XYZ charge account has been declined for the following reasons:

_____ Credit application incomplete
_____ Insufficient number of credit references provided
_____ Unacceptable type of credit references provided
_____ Unable to verify credit references
_____ Temporary or irregular employment
_____ Unable to verify employment
_____ Length of employment
_____ Income insufficient for amount of credit requested
_____ Excessive obligations in relation to income
_____ Unable to verify income
_____ Length of residence
_____ Temporary residence
_____ Unable to verify residence
_____ No credit file
_____ Limited credit experience
_____ Poor credit performance with us
_____ Delinquent past or present credit obligations with others
_____ Garnishment, attachment, foreclosure, repossession, collection action, or judgment

_____ Bankruptcy
_____ Value or type of collateral not sufficient
_____ Other: _____

In determining your creditworthiness, we relied, in whole or in part, on information provided to us by the following credit-reporting agency:

_____

_____

_____

Under the Fair Credit Reporting Act, you have the right to know the information contained in your credit file. Any questions regarding such information should be directed to the credit-reporting agency above.

NOTICE: The federal Equal Credit Opportunity Act prohibits creditors from discriminating against credit applicants on the basis of race, color, religion, national origin, sex, marital status, or age (provided the applicant has the capacity to enter into a binding contract); because all or part of the applicant's income derives from any public assistance program; or because the applicant has in good faith exercised any right under the Consumer Protection Act. The federal agency that administers compliance with this law concerning this creditor is: _____.

Appealing Adverse Credit Decisions

If you believe a credit application was unfairly rejected, you should appeal the decision with the credit grantor. Identify and focus your efforts toward the person or persons who make credit-granting decisions. For local credit grantors, make a personal appeal to the credit-granting person. If a credit committee was responsible for your rejection, ask to make a presentation to this committee. In most cases, it is best to write a letter detailing the reasons why you believe the original rejection decision should be reevaluated. By filing an appeal with the creditor, you personalize what is normally a very impersonal process. Your tenacity also demonstrates to the creditor your confidence in yourself and your repayment capabilities.

If you suspect the rejection violates your rights under the Equal Credit Opportunity Act (for example, your request for credit was denied because of your race), alert the creditor to your knowledge of the law and your rights under it.

Also, provide the creditor with any additional information that might enhance your chances for approval. For example, if your credit history is scant, bring evidence of favorable credit experiences, like former accounts, accounts under former names, accounts at previous addresses, or paid bills. Or substantiate assets by bringing in recent bank statements, a copy of the deed to your house, a copy of your most recent tax return, evidence of income from different sources, or similar documentation.

Do not be belligerent with a creditor when appealing an adverse credit decision. Your best approach is to be deferential and to appear as reasonable and responsible as possible.

Protection Against Credit Discrimination

The federal Equal Credit Opportunity Act (ECOA) assures everyone an equal chance to receive credit. This act does not entitle you to receive credit simply because you apply for it. It just prohibits creditors from discriminating against certain classes of people. Creditors are still free to evaluate applications based on your income, debts, credit history, or other criteria they may select—so long as their criteria do not violate ECOA.

ECOA prohibits discrimination against you on a credit application because of your:

- Age
- Sex
- Marital status
- Religion
- Race
- Color
- National origin

You also cannot be denied credit because you:

- Receive public assistance
- Exercised rights under the federal consumer credit laws

The Equal Credit Opportunity Act's protections apply to any creditor who regularly extends credit or anyone who participates in a credit-granting decision. Thus, financial institutions (banks, savings and loans, credit unions), department stores, credit card companies, finance and loan companies, mortgage companies, travel companies (gasoline, airline charge cards), and the like are covered by the law. Also, anyone who arranges financing, such as a real estate or loan broker, is bound by the act.

Under the ECOA, creditors cannot discourage you from applying for a loan or extension of credit because of any of the above factors. Nor can a creditor ask for your sex, race, national origin, or religion (although, in some circumstances, you may be asked to divulge this information voluntarily). If you are applying for your own unsecured accounts, creditors generally cannot inquire about your marital status (in community-property states creditors are permitted to obtain this information) unless your spouse has some direct involvement in the account (that is, if your spouse will be using the account or the spouse's income is used to obtain the credit). Creditors may ask if you receive alimony, child support, or separate maintenance payments, provided you are informed that you don't have to reveal such information unless you are relying on such income for the extension of credit. Creditors are also free to ask if you have to make such court-ordered payments.

Creditors cannot consider your age, unless you are under the legal age for entering into a binding contract (eighteen to twenty-one, depending on state law) or are sixty-two and older. Under the ECOA creditors cannot fault, but rather must favor, applicants who are sixty-two and older. Creditors may take into consideration whether you have a phone in your home, but they cannot consider whether the phone is in your name. If you wish to borrow money to purchase or improve a house, creditors cannot consider your race or that of the people in the house's neighborhood.

Creditors must also give all forms of income the same weight. Thus, a man's income cannot be given greater weight than a woman's, creditors cannot refuse to consider consistently received alimony or reliable public assistance income, nor can they refuse to consider part-time, pension, annuity, or retirement benefit income.

If you believe any creditor has violated the Equal Credit Opportunity Act concerning a credit application you filed, consult appendix 1, "How to Enforce Your Rights."

CHAPTER 2

Protecting Yourself on Current Obligations

Staying Current on Obligations

The best way to protect yourself on current obligations is to make timely payments, according to the terms of your credit agreements. Make every effort to get your payments mailed or delivered to your creditors by their due date. To allow for any delays, send your payments a couple of days prior to their due date. This should protect you against being assessed a late payment fee as well as assuring the favorable reporting of your account with credit-reporting agencies.

Follow your creditors' instructions concerning how, when, and where to make bill payments. Make sure your payments are mailed or delivered to the address indicated for receipt of payments by your creditor. If you pay by check, write your account number on the check. If you do not have a payment stub or detachable portion of a bill to return with your payment, jot a note to your creditor indicating the date, amount of the payment attached, your account number, and your name and address.

If you suspect you are going to be late on a payment, consider calling your creditor. Explain the reasons for your tardiness, giving the date by which the creditor should expect payment. If possible, try to make at least a partial payment by the due date. The remainder of the payment should be made as quickly as possible.

When your statement arrives, check promptly to make sure your payments have been properly credited to your account. If there are any problems, file a billing dispute with your creditor to have the payment credited.

Setting Repayment Priorities

You will obviously want to repay all legitimate, current debts according to your agreements. You should probably try to meet these obligations as quickly as possible (since time is money on credit obligations), with all creditors being treated fairly in the process. You should also be on the lookout for the following:

Obligations That Contain Hidden Costs

Because some obligations contain hidden costs, such as late payment charges and over-the-limit fees, these types of obligations should be a top priority. You should make every effort to avoid such extraordinary, additional costs.

Late Payment Charges.   If you are being assessed late payment charges, try to submit payments before the due date. If you're cutting it close, contact the creditor to determine the monthly date when payments must be received in order to avoid these charges. This date, which varies among creditors, is normally a certain number of days beyond the payment due date. For example, while some creditors may assess late payment charges on the payment due date, most give a five- to ten-day grace period beyond the payment due date for payments to be received and credited to an account. Once your creditor's policy is determined, make every effort to ensure that your payments are credited by this date. If you cannot make a payment until the date on which the fee will be assessed, if possible, hand deliver rather than mail, the payment to your creditor.

Over-the-Limit Fees. If you are being charged an over-the-limit fee, try to bring your indebtedness below your approved credit limit. Should you have difficulty accomplishing this, you should determine the balance beyond which this fee is assessed. Some creditors assess an over-the-limit fee if you go a penny beyond the credit limit; others charge if your balance exceeds your credit limit by 15 percent. Once this point has been determined, make every effort to bring your balance below this point, and strive to bring your indebtedness below your approved credit limit. If you are unable to do this, contact the creditor to request that your credit limit be increased to the level of your current balance, so further over-the-limit fees can be avoided. If this is done, assure the creditor that account balances will remain below the revised credit limit.

Obligations at High Rates of Interest

Interest rates have declined in recent years. However, many people continue to pay high interest rates—18 percent and more—on some credit obligations. You should list all your credit obligations, including the rate of interest on each. Then, repay those debts with the highest rates of interest first. The sooner you are able to pay them off, the less money they will cost you. If you have several obligations with rates of interest in excess of 15 percent, you might consider taking out a lower-interest loan to repay these obligations (see chapter 8).

Tax Consequences of Consumer Debt

Prior to the 1986 tax reform, if you itemized deductions on your federal income tax return, you could deduct 100 percent of the consumer interest payments you made during the tax year. Consumer interest is interest paid on obligations such as credit cards, personal loans, automobile loans, student loans, department store charges, and the like. This meant that if you were overextended or carried a sizable amount of consumer debt, you obtained tax relief at the end of the year through the full deductibility of consumer interest payments.

Tax reform has dramatically changed the rules concerning the deductibility of consumer interest. *The consumer interest deduction will be phased out entirely by the beginning of 1991.* Consumer interest deductions will be (or have been) allowed according to the following schedule:

> 1986—100%
> 1987— 65%
> 1988— 40%
> 1989— 20%
> 1990— 10%
> 1991— 0%

For example, under the 1986 tax reform rules, $500 consumer interest payments would yield allowable deductions of:

> 1986—$500 ($500 × 100%)
> 1987—$325 ($500 × 65%)

1988—$200 ($500 × 40%)
1989—$100 ($500 × 20%)
1990—$ 50 ($500 × 10%)
1991—$ 0 ($500 × 0%)

Since the deductibility of consumer interest will soon be phased out, pay off all consumer debt as quickly as possible.

If you have outstanding credit obligations, are financially responsible, and own a home and have amassed equity in it, you might consider a home equity loan as a way of restructuring your indebtedness for tax purposes (see the "Home Equity Loan" section in chapter 8).

Resolving Billing Disputes

Have you ever found a charge on your monthly credit card bill for an item you did not purchase? Has your account ever not been credited for items you returned or did not receive from a merchant? Has your statement ever reflected incorrect charges or duplicate charges (the same charge reflected twice)? Have you ever made a payment that was never credited to your account?

Should any of these ever happen to you, you must quickly assert your rights with your creditor to have the matter resolved. There is no reason for you to pay or be penalized for someone else's billing mistake. You should become familiar with your protections under the federal Fair Credit Billing Act.

You should carefully scrutinize your monthly billing statements from creditors. You simply cannot take your creditor's accounting on your statement at face value. Billing errors occur. People make mistakes, and so do computers. Thus, you must routinely review each of your billing statements when it is received, comparing your copies of receipts with the charges reflected on your statement. If you notice an error, take the steps indicated below.

The federal Fair Credit Billing Act entitles you to specific rights in the event of a billing dispute on open-end credit accounts (like store charge cards, credit cards, and lines of credit [for example, overdraft protection on a bank account]). The act does not apply if you have a billing dispute on closed-end credit obligations (obligations paid in fixed amounts on a fixed payment schedule until the amount is paid in full, such as mortgages, car loans, personal loans, and the like).

While a telephone call to your creditor might be helpful, such a call will *not* preserve your rights under the Fair Credit Billing Act. To preserve these rights, you must write your creditor within sixty days of your receipt of a billing statement containing an error. Do not simply send your letter of dispute along with your payment. Rather, mail your letter separately to the address indicated on your statement for billing disputes (and not directly to the store unless this is indicated). In your letter, make sure to:

- Include your name, address, and account number
- Indicate your belief that your statement contains a billing error
- Identify the amount of the billing error, and
- State your reasons for believing a billing error exists

If you wish, send *copies* of documentation verifying your billing error assertions (for example, sales slips or cancelled checks) to your creditor. Keep the originals for your files. To establish proof of mailing and receipt of your letter, you might also consider using certified mail, return receipt requested.

On receipt of your letter identifying a billing error, your creditor must do the following:

- Acknowledge receipt of your letter within thirty days
- Conduct a reasonable investigation within two billing cycles (but not longer than ninety days) and do either of the following:

  1. Make appropriate corrections to your account (including the crediting of finance charges on amounts erroneously billed). Your creditor must send you a letter explaining the corrections to be made on your account.
  2. Send you an explanation setting forth the reasons why a billing error does not exist or the reasons why you still owe a portion of the disputed amount. At your request, the creditor must furnish you with copies of any documents on which such determinations were based.

During these periods, you do not have to pay the amount in dispute, including finance charges and minimum payments relating to the matter in dispute. You must, however, make other payments required under your credit agreement on charges not in dispute.

While the dispute is being resolved, your creditor may not initiate collection activities against you concerning the amount of the billing error. However, during these periods, creditors are free to collect amounts that are *not* the subject of dispute. In addition, your creditor may not restrict or close your account (before sending you a written explanation as to why a billing error does not exist) *solely* because of your failure to pay the amount you found to be in error. The disputed amount may, however, be counted toward your credit limit.

The Fair Credit Billing Act protects your credit report during a billing error dispute. This law prohibits a creditor or a creditor's agent from directly or indirectly threatening to make an adverse report to a credit-reporting agency because of your failure to make payment of the amount of your billing dispute. However, once the creditor notifies you of the reasons why a billing error does not exist, the creditor may—after you have been allowed at least ten days to make payment—report the delinquent account to credit-reporting agencies. Should you appeal your creditor's initial decision that a billing error does not exist, your creditor may report the account as delinquent to credit-reporting agencies so long as the amount in dispute is indicated and you are notified of the names and addresses of the parties to whom the delinquency is being reported.

If your creditor fails to follow these procedures, the right to collect the amount in dispute, including any finance charges relating to the disputed amount, up to $50 is forfeited. This is true even if it is later determined that the bill does not contain a billing error. If you believe your creditor has failed to live up to obligations under the Fair Credit Billing Act, consult appendix 1, "How to Enforce Your Rights."

Protection Against Defective Merchandise

Suppose you purchase merchandise that turns out to be defective or of inferior quality. Your first step, obviously, is to take the merchandise back to the place where you bought it and give the seller the opportunity to either replace the item or refund your money. You must make a good-faith effort to obtain satisfactory resolution of the disagreement or problem from the seller.

To protect yourself, chronicle the actions you take to get the matter resolved. Record the dates, times, and nature of communications with the seller concerning the merchandise. Write down the names and phone numbers of everyone you speak with. It might be helpful to write a letter to the merchant detailing your concern over the quality of the merchandise and the steps you feel the merchant should take to resolve the conflict.

What do you do if the merchant refuses? If you paid by cash or check, you might want to pursue your rights under your state's laws. If you made the purchase with a credit card, you may be entitled to additional rights under the Fair Credit Billing Act. In such cases, your rights will still be determined by the laws of the state in which you live; however, the Fair Credit Billing Act may extend these state provisions.

Under the act, you may be allowed to enforce the same legal actions against your credit card issuer that you have under state law against the seller of the merchandise. For example, if your state law allows you to withhold payment to a seller of defective merchandise, under the Fair Credit Billing Act—if you meet certain criteria—you might also be able to withhold payment to your credit card issuer. Thus, you should first determine what defenses-to-payment protections are afforded under your state's laws. You might then be able to assert these state-allowed defenses against both the seller and the credit card issuer.

If you purchased the item from a company that also financed the purchase (for example, you bought an item at Sears and charged it on your Sears charge card), since the seller is also the credit card issuer, you need only assert your rights once. However, if you did *not* purchase the item from the company providing credit (for example, you make a purchase at Sears but pay with MasterCard), to be able to assert state-provided defenses against both the seller and the credit card issuer, you must meet the following requirements:

- You must have purchased the item in your home state or within 100 miles of your current billing address
- The amount of the purchase must be greater than $50

Protecting Yourself Against Credit and Charge Card Theft and Fraud

Have you ever had a credit card transaction declined and later discovered that your credit limit had been eaten up by a series of unauthorized charges on your card? After the loss or theft of your wallet or pocketbook, have you had to cancel all your credit cards? Have you noticed unauthorized charges on your monthly bill? Have you ever received a phone call in which the caller asked you to give him or her your credit card number?

If your credit or charge cards are lost or stolen, *immediately* notify your credit card issuers. Most have toll-free numbers and twenty-four-hour service available for this purpose. You should follow up with a telegram or letter advising your creditor in writing of the loss or theft. In this correspondence, indicate your name and card number, the precise time and date you discovered your card was missing, and the time and date you reported the lost or stolen card to your creditor.

Under the federal Truth-In-Lending Act, you cannot be held responsible for any charges made on your cards *after* you have reported them lost or stolen. Even though your maximum liability can never exceed fifty dollars per card, the earlier you act, the greater the likelihood you will be able to limit your out-of-pocket expenses and the unauthorized user's access to your credit. Also, if several credit cards were lost or stolen, your maximum liability can quickly mount up. Since some homeowner's and renter's insurance policies contain liability coverage for credit card thefts, you should consult your policies for possible reimbursement of out-of-pocket expenses.

After reporting a credit or charge card loss or theft, review your billing statements carefully. Should any unauthorized charges appear, follow the procedures outlined in the preceding "Billing Errors" section.

Some credit card fraud is more discreet than an obvious theft. For example, someone may gain access to one of your credit card account numbers and slip a couple of charges onto your bill. The only way you can catch this type of fraud is to open your billing statements promptly and carefully scrutinize them. Compare these statements against receipts and your records of account activities. If, when reviewing your monthly statement, you notice any unauthorized charges on your billing statement, you should take the steps in the preceding section on "Resolving Billing Disputes." If there is a large number of unauthorized charges or it becomes apparent that such unauthorized charges reflect an ongoing problem, cancel the card and have a new one issued.

To protect yourself against these and other types of credit card theft and fraud problems, take these precautions:

• Make sure to sign new credit cards when you get them.

• Keep all your credit card account numbers, expiration dates, and card-issuer phone numbers and addresses in one easily accessible, safe place so you will be able to immediately respond in the event of loss or theft. You might consider buying a subscription to one of the many card registration services that, with one easy phone call, will cancel all your credit cards and request that new ones be issued.

• Keep your credit cards in a safe place when not in use. Since you can usually anticipate your spending needs, do not routinely carry all of your credit cards. Rather, if you know you may go to a particular store and wish to make a purchase, take your store charge card with you. Then immediately remove it from your wallet or pocketbook when you return.

• Watch your card when you give it to a salesperson. Make sure it is only used for your transaction; be certain the card you receive back is yours; put your card in a safe place immediately on its return (for example, do not leave it on the counter while the clerk is packaging your purchase). Keep an eye on your wallet or pocketbook while the clerk is processing your transaction.

• Carefully scrutinize the charge slip. Is your account number reflected? Are *all* the amounts listed (usually there are handwritten as well as printed totals) correct? Draw a line through any blank spaces where additional amounts might be inserted. Avoid signing a blank, imprinted credit card sales slip.

• If carbons are used with your transaction, make sure to tear them up. If the clerk makes a mistake and has to redo the charge slip, make certain the first paperwork is destroyed in your presence.

• Be careful with what happens to your copies of credit card receipts once you get them home. Never simply toss them in the trash. Make certain to tear them up before discarding them. Do not leave credit cards or receipts lying around your home or workplace. Keep them in a safe place, out of view.

• Never give your credit card number to anyone over the phone unless you initiate the call. Should you be enticed by the offering of someone who calls you, ask the caller to put the offering in writing and to provide you with either an address or phone number where you can contact them. If you are not familiar with a particular company, call your local consumer protection office, Better Business Bureau, or your state attorney general's office before ordering.

• If you initiate a call and give your credit card number to someone over the phone, be discreet. Do not allow anyone within earshot to overhear your number.

• Make sure to notify your credit card companies promptly of a change of address.

• Never lend your credit or charge cards or give your account numbers to anyone else to use.

• Never write your account number on a postcard, the outside of a letter, your office Rolodex, or any such place. When mailing your payments, make certain your account number is not visible through the envelope.

Protecting Yourself Against Automatic Teller Machine (ATM) Fraud

The above recommendations should also be helpful in protecting yourself against ATM (automatic teller machine or electronic banking machine) fraud. For ATM cards, keep the following recommendations in mind:

• Do not write your personal identification number (PIN) on your ATM card or on anything else you keep in your wallet or pocketbook.

• Select a PIN that is different from other numbers that may be present in your wallet or pocketbook (such as your birthdate, address, phone number, or social security number).

• Memorize your PIN.

• Never give your PIN to anyone else.

• Be careful not to allow anyone to discover your PIN through watching your ATM use.

• Never write your PIN on a postcard, the outside of an envelope, a deposit slip, or your office Rolodex.

- Immediately examine all ATM receipts and bank statements.

In the event of ATM fraud, your rights are governed by the federal Electronic Funds Transfer Act. Under this act:

- If you report your ATM card missing *before* it is used without your permission, you are not responsible for any unauthorized use of the card
- If an unauthorized use occurs and you report the card missing within two days after you notice its loss, your maximum liability cannot exceed fifty dollars,
- If an unauthorized use occurs and you do *not* report the card missing within two days after you notice its loss, your maximum liability jumps to $500
- If an unauthorized use occurs and you do *not* report the card missing within sixty days after your bank statement is mailed to you, you could lose all your remaining balance in the account, along with any available line of credit for overdraft protection you may have attached to your account.

Since your out-of-pocket expenses are reduced through the earliest notification of your financial institution, contact the bank immediately on learning of the loss. Remember, once you report the loss of your ATM card, you cannot be held responsible for any future unauthorized transactions on it.

CHAPTER 3

Do You Have a Credit Problem?

To determine if you have a credit problem, study the sections that follow.

Credit Danger Signals

Financial problems do not happen overnight. Everyone needs to be able to recognize and be on the lookout for signals that could warn of impending credit danger.

Which items apply to you?

	Yes	No
Do you spend more and more of your monthly take-home income to pay bills?	_____	_____
Are you near, at, or over the limit on your lines of credit?	_____	_____
Are you extending repayment schedules—paying in sixty or ninety days bills that you once paid in thirty?	_____	_____

	Yes	No
Are you chronically late in paying your bills?	_____	_____
Do you routinely pay late penalties on outstanding credit obligations?	_____	_____
Can you only make the minimum payments on your revolving charge accounts?	_____	_____
Are you paying bills with money earmarked for something else?	_____	_____
Are you borrowing to pay for items you used to be able to pay for yourself?	_____	_____
Are you paying half your bills one month and half the next?	_____	_____
Do you find it necessary to write post-dated checks?	_____	_____
Do you charge small, miscellaneous, and recreation expenses because you don't have the money to pay for them?	_____	_____
Do you find yourself using credit to meet ordinary, day-to-day living expenses?	_____	_____
Do you often find yourself "overshopping" to meet minimum-purchase requirements for charge card transactions?	_____	_____
Do you often worry that credit card transactions will be declined?	_____	_____
Are you tapping your savings to pay current bills?	_____	_____
Is your savings cushion inadequate or nonexistent?	_____	_____

	Yes	No
Do you take out a new loan before the old one is paid off, or take out a new one to pay off the old loan?	____	____
Do you put off medical and dental visits because you can't afford them right now?	____	____
Have you cancelled auto, medical, or life insurance to make ends meet?	____	____
Are you working overtime or moonlighting to meet current financial obligations?	____	____
Are you living beyond your means?	____	____
If you lost your job, would you be in immediate financial difficulty?	____	____
Are you chronically overdrawn at the bank?	____	____
Do you routinely receive mail and/or telephone calls from creditors regarding unpaid bills or late payments?	____	____
Are you threatened with repossession of your car or credit cards, or with other legal action?	____	____
Have you had credit cards taken away from you by creditors?	____	____
Do you have any negative marks on your credit rating?	____	____
Have you been denied credit because of an adverse report from a credit-reporting agency?	____	____
Have you been denied credit because of overextension of credit obligations?	____	____

	Yes	No
Are you unable to estimate how much you owe in installment debts?	___	___
Do you worry a lot about money?	___	___
Do your monthly installment payments exceed 20 percent of your monthly take-home pay?	___	___

Source: Derived from *Managing Your Credit,* a booklet published by Money Management Institute (Prospect Heights, IL: Household Finance Corporation, 1987).

Your results should be evaluated as follows:

• If none of the items applies to you, you should still be aware of the warning signals, review them occasionally, and be able to recognize behavior before it becomes a problem.

• A yes to any single item should not cause alarm. It could simply be an indication that you should be cautious and on the lookout for other credit danger signals.

• If several of the items apply to you, you may be experiencing credit difficulty or be precariously close to it. If you fall into this category, immediate action should be taken. Carefully review the chapters that follow. Depending on the size of your problem, you may need to curtail your spending, develop a budget, or negotiate repayment plans with your creditors.

How Much Do You Owe?

To determine the extent of your current indebtedness, list all creditors to whom you owe money. Make sure to include all debts, regardless of how old they may be. After each debt has been listed, add all outstanding current balances to determine your total indebtedness.

Name of Creditor/Type of Loan	*Current Outstanding Balance*
_____	$_____
_____	$_____
_____	$_____
_____	$_____
_____	$_____
_____	$_____
_____	$_____
_____	$_____
_____	$_____
_____	$_____
Total Indebtedness	$_____

Tolerable Limits on Credit Obligations

The most significant warning signal of credit danger is debts that exceed tolerable limits. In other words, your debt-to-income ratio should not be out of balance. You need to be able to recognize the break points that indicate overextension of credit obligations.

Your installment debts (like automobile loans, credit cards, store charge accounts, personal loans, or student loans) should not exceed more than 20 percent of your annual take-home pay. Anything in excess of 20 percent is generally considered an overextension on credit obligations. While 20 percent represents the tolerable maximum, a 15 percent limit is recommended as a more comfortable level of indebtedness. At 15 percent, your debts will be more manageable than at a higher rate and you will have greater flexibility in meeting any unplanned or sudden expenditures.

The chart below indicates tolerable limits on credit obligations for different income levels. You should determine your income level and identify your "comfortable" and "maximum" credit obligation amounts. These should then be compared with the actual amount of your total indebtedness.

SUGGESTED INCOME TO DEBT RATIOS BY INCOME LEVEL

TAKE HOME PAY		Comfortable	Maximum
Per Month	Per Year	15%	20%
$ 250	$ 3,000	$ 450	$ 600
$ 500	$ 6,000	$ 900	$1,200
$ 750	$ 9,000	$1,350	$1,800
$1,000	$12,000	$1,800	$2,400
$1,250	$15,000	$2,250	$3,000
$1,500	$18,000	$2,700	$3,600
$1,750	$21,000	$3,150	$4,200
$2,000	$24,000	$3,600	$4,800
$2,250	$27,000	$4,050	$5,400
$2,500	$30,000	$4,500	$6,000
$2,750	$33,000	$4,950	$6,600
$3,000	$36,000	$5,400	$7,200
$3,250	$39,000	$5,850	$7,800
$3,500	$42,000	$6,300	$8,400
$3,750	$45,000	$6,750	$9,000

Once your percentages have been determined, they should be evaluated as follows:

• If you exceed the 20 percent level, you should make every effort to bring your total indebtedness down to or below the maximum tolerable amount for your income category.

• If you are between the 15 percent and 20 percent levels, you should not assume any new credit obligations and strive toward the lower goal.

• If you fall below 15 percent, you probably are not overextended. However, you should become familiar with the tolerable limits on credit obligations for your income category and be wary of any obligations that would force you to become overextended.

The 15 percent and 20 percent limits are flexible and are intended only as guidelines for assessing general credit conditions. Your own specific situation should be taken into consideration when applying the guidelines. For example, if you just purchased a new car, your indebtedness might well exceed the tolerable guidelines set forth in the chart.

What Type of Debtor Are You?

• *Responsible debtors* are cautious with credit, keeping obligations within reason and paying all bills in a timely fashion.
• *Situational debtors* have gotten into credit difficulty as the result of unpredictable or unusual circumstances. They may progress through different stages of credit difficulty, depending upon the magnitude of the problem.
• *Chronic debtors* are powerless over credit, compulsive or impulsive spenders, unable to handle credit or to manage financial affairs. Spending behavior represents a continuing or prolonged problem.
• *Hybrid debtors* have characteristics of situational and chronic debtors, usually through the presence of primary and secondary addictive behaviors.

Responsible Debtors

If you choose to use credit, you should strive to be a responsible debtor. If you fall into this category, you should become aware of the credit danger signals and tolerable limits on credit obligations so you will be able to recognize and deal with a problem before it becomes too big.

Situational Debtors

Almost everyone has the potential of becoming a situational debtor at some time in his or her life. A major event or crisis—the birth of a child, an illness, death in the family, accidents, medical problems, loss of a job, legal problems, business difficulties, drinking, and drug dependencies—can throw even responsible debtors into credit difficulty.

If you are a situational debtor, your credit problems will be totally and directly attributable to a readily identifiable cause. Once the situation that caused your credit problems has been brought under control, your credit problems should stabilize. You may simply need to make amends for your past spending activities.

If, on the other hand, you find that new debts—those incurred after the situation has been resolved—are creating your credit problems, you may discover that you are a compulsive spender (chronic debtor).

Chronic Debtors

Some people simply cannot control their spending. Compulsive or impulsive spenders, they are addicted to spending and unable to handle credit or manage financial affairs. A chronic debtor is as powerless over spending as an alcoholic is over drinking. Routine overspending, unplanned and sometimes unwanted purchases, a continuing inability to make timely payments on credit obligations, an ongoing lack of adequate planning, and prolonged financial irresponsibility may point to a chronic debtor.

Assistance is available for chronic debtors. If you suspect you are a chronic debtor or are concerned about someone who is, you should consider investigating Debtors Anonymous, a program for chronic debtors based on the principles and structure of Alcoholics Anonymous. Attendance is free, although a voluntary contribution is requested. Debtors Anonymous groups are listed in the white pages of your local telephone directory.

In addition, chronic debtors can be treated professionally through outpatient psychiatric or psychological care. This type of treatment may be expensive. Information on health-care professionals who specialize in spending-addiction problems can be obtained from your family physician, your local community mental health center, professional medical societies, or the yellow pages of your local telephone directory.

Hybrid Debtors

Many debtors are situational and chronic at the same time. For example, assume that your financial problems are the direct result of some type of compulsive behavior, such as a drinking problem that is draining your financial resources. If, after dealing with your drinking problem, it becomes apparent that your spending practices are also unmanageable, you may be suffering from parallel addictions.

In such a case, you will need to deal with both types of compulsive behaviors. Since it may be difficult to tackle both of these problems at the same time, you should identify your more severe form of compulsive behavior and deal with it as your primary addiction. Other types of compulsive behaviors must also be dealt with, but as secondary addictions.

CHAPTER 4

The Psychology of Credit Problems

Identifying and Dealing with the Causes of Your Credit Problems

Whether you are a situational, chronic, or hybrid debtor, to address your credit difficulties effectively, the underlying activity or behavior that contributed to the problem must first be recognized and then resolved or brought under control.

You must assess realistically what caused your credit problems. For example, suppose you routinely gamble away every penny you can get your fingers on. To manage your financial affairs effectively, you must first come to terms with your gambling behavior. Similarly, if unemployment has caused your financial woes, since it's hard to get blood out of a turnip, you may have to find another job or take on a part-time job temporarily to make ends meet, before your financial troubles can be addressed.

The causes of financial troubles are not always so readily identifiable. Suppose you have a weight problem, are single and looking for a partner, or are trapped in a job you absolutely hate. To compensate for your frustrations or feelings of inadequacy, you may spend money, sometimes excessively. Spending money may be your way of venting anxieties over a variety of circumstances in your life. It may be an antidepressant. Spending money may be an enjoyable way of killing time or relieving boredom on an otherwise uneventful afternoon. It may serve as a substitute for things that are missing in your life, such as love or companionship. Spending money can also make you feel important or secure. Thus, spending money may be your way of bolstering self-esteem in response to unrelated, difficult situations.

Carefully evaluate the role money plays in your life and try to recognize your motivations for spending it. If you find yourself in one of the above situations, since the underlying problem is probably not financial in nature, a financial solution is hardly going to resolve your dilemma. Rather, money simply represents a "quick fix" and nothing more than a Band-Aid on a far more painful wound. Spending money may simply be easier than dealing with complex, troubling, often highly emotional problems. Only by dealing with underlying problems can your greater anxieties be resolved. In the examples above, instead of spending money, you should address head-on the root causes of the frustration (that is, go on a diet, place yourself in situations in which you might meet a partner, or look for a new job). Do not rely on money to solve these emotional problems for you.

It is ironic that for many people with credit problems, spending practices arose out of an attempt to shore up sagging self-esteem. To cope with a variety of problems, some people resort to spending as a means of temporarily propping themselves up. However, if this spending behavior becomes a problem in and of itself, it only undermines further the spender's self-esteem. So, if you find yourself spending to overcome problems in another area of your life, be very careful not to fall prey to this Catch-22.

Accepting Responsibility for Your Credit Problems

The first step you must take toward solving your credit problems is to acknowledge their existence. For many people recognition of the problem is the most difficult step. However, it is far more preferable to acknowledge and deal with a problem than to allow it to continue.

You must also accept full responsibility for these problems. You are responsible for your actions and your debts. While you, personally, have a lot at stake in resolving your credit difficulties, there may be others—spouse, children, dependent parents—who share the repercussions of these problems. Unless you have a rich uncle die, marry money, or win the lottery, the chances are pretty good that if you don't solve your credit problems, nobody else will.

Don't be surprised if, after accepting responsibility for your credit problems, you feel overwhelmed by them. You may have juggled sizable credit problems for years, with little or no concern about the impact of such irresponsibility. Your irresponsibility helped you not to care, not to worry.

By accepting responsibility for your credit problems, you begin to care. You begin to realize that you have to deal with these problems and that your irresponsible days are behind you. You may simply have to dig yourself out of the hole you have dug for yourself.

It just doesn't seem fair that by accepting responsibility for your credit problems, you are confronted with debts which are the product of years of irresponsibility. While your life would obviously be a lot simpler were it not for your past debts, you must never underestimate the valuable lesson that irresponsibility has taught you. By having to work through your credit problems, often over a couple of years, you will be reminded of the repercussions of your past spending indiscretions. And, once you have regained firm financial footing, you will, no doubt, have benefited from the lesson you have learned. You will probably have gained a healthier respect for the value of the dollar, become prudent in your future use of credit, and changed your spending habits for life.

Restoring Your Self-Esteem

Financial problems can easily destroy your self-esteem. Many people with credit problems find their self-esteem either nonexistent or at an all-time low. The fact that creditors may be contacting you about past-due bills may underscore your negative feelings about yourself.

By accepting responsibility for your credit problems, you are taking a positive step toward correcting a major concern in your life. Soon, you will be able to see tangible results. This should make you feel good about yourself, and will help to restore some of the self-esteem you may have lost during the worst days of your credit difficulties. You can take pride in the fact you are transforming a negative in your life into something positive.

To bolster your self-esteem, seek out activities that make you feel good about yourself. Take pride in doing things like paying your bills, sticking to your budget, living economically, finding ways to save money, forgoing purchases, restoring your credit rating, and so on. Also, look to other, nonfinancial areas of your life for activities that make you feel good about yourself. There are probably many of them. Start trying to accentuate the positives—the good things—about yourself. Deal with the negatives, but don't allow them to taint or control your impression of yourself. Be proud of your attributes and work toward improvement.

After a brief period of dealing with credit problems, most people start enjoying being responsible. Your self-perception changes from that of an irresponsible person to that of a responsible person. You'll grow to appreciate that the positive rewards of responsibility are far more lasting than the fleeting satisfactions of your irresponsible days.

Accepting Change

Departing from the status quo can be quite traumatic. But breaking old habits and establishing new ones is the best way to deal with problems created by past behaviors. You must be willing to accept change as an integral part of your attempts to deal with your credit problems.

If your problems are significant, accepting change may be relatively easy for you. Your problems may be so big that you have reached your wits' end or "bottomed out." You may simply have grown tired of dealing with nuances of the same problem. In such instances, anything may be better than your current situation.

For many others, accepting change may be more difficult since choices may not be so clear-cut. The need for change may be shrouded in feelings of indifference or complacency. You may have become relatively comfortable in uncomfortable situations. Or you may prefer to deal with the security represented by the status quo, rather than taking chances with the unknown.

For example, a spouse may endure a lackluster marriage rather than get a divorce and face the cold, cruel world alone. Despite the marriage's shortcomings, it is a known quantity one has learned to cope with. Divorce, on the other hand, represents a tremendous change that some are unwilling to confront.

There may also be some very compelling, practical reasons for thwarting change. Alone, the spouse may not be able to support the kind of life-style enjoyed during the marriage. Relationships with friends and family, which grew out of the marriage, may be jeopardized. Change may create some big complications, such as where to live, what to do with the kids or the house, and who gets the dog.

Change can be both terrifying and exciting. While it may represent the ending of one chapter in your life, it also signals the beginning of a new one. Since the future sometimes comes a little before you may be ready to give up your grasp on the present, change may represent your opportunity to confront your future head-on.

Change is essential to allow you to move on, to approach new and different challenges. These new experiences sometimes lead to far greater, unanticipated rewards. Thus, if you are willing to take a chance with change, you can broaden your future horizons.

You may well have developed a series of defense mechanisms designed to thwart emerging notions of changes in your current behavior. Defense mechanisms can be firmly entrenched behaviors that allow you to continue old practices.

Your defense mechanisms may allow you to come up with any number of rationalizations designed to perpetuate a particular type of behavior. You may toy with the notion of change but limit your options or "stack the deck" so your only logical response is to return to the status quo. You may blame the repercussions of your activities on someone else or events outside your control, thereby insulating yourself from blame. You may fear that you will be unable to tackle your problem successfully, so you might decide not even to deal with it. You may fantasize that things are not as bad as they might seem, that someone will rescue you from your problems, or that they will miraculously disappear.

Before you can change such behaviors, you must first become aware of the defense mechanisms you use. Be wary of any activities designed to perpetuate the behavior in question. Since you may need help in identifying your defense mechanisms, have a family member or friend point them out to you as they occur.

Only by breaking through your defense mechanisms will you be able to change your old behavior patterns. Once defense mechanisms are recognized and dealt with, new behavior patterns can be adopted. Old destructive behaviors can then be replaced by new constructive behaviors.

Since you may be dealing in unknown territory, it is important that you remain open-minded. You must not close your mind to or distrust concepts simply because they may be new to you. You must be open to fresh, new ideas and approaches to your problems and must not remain wedded to old notions. After all, didn't your past activities help to create your dilemma in the first place? Just take it easy and give change a chance.

Change often allows you to take a proactive rather than a reactive approach to your problems. Seize the initiative, map out your future courses of action rather than simply responding to problems as they arise. And take pride in your resolve to deal with your problems.

Dealing with Worry

Your credit difficulties may represent very serious problems. But you can't make yourself sick over them or lie awake at night worrying about them. You simply cannot take your debts so seriously that worrying about them becomes a problem in and of itself.

One of your best resources when dealing with worry will probably arise naturally out of dealing with your credit problems. After a repayment plan has been established, your worries should subside. There is no reason to worry— just so long as you make the agreed-upon payments. If you stay current in your payments, creditors won't hassle you. Since you have done all that you can do, for the time being, to resolve your credit difficulties, don't allow yourself to agonize over or dwell on these problems any more. It may just be a matter of time before you can satisfy your outstanding credit obligations.

Talking About Your Credit Problems

There is no reason for you to endure your credit problems privately. In order to maintain a healthier, more balanced outlook toward these difficulties, you should routinely discuss them with family members, relatives, close friends, clergy, health-care professionals, trained financial counselors, or others who, like you, are experiencing credit difficulty.

By talking about these problems, you provide yourself with an outlet to vent your frustrations instead of letting them fester within you. Talking about your problems also affords you the opportunity to share your accomplishments and to benefit from the experiences, suggestions, and advice of others. You can bounce ideas off your confidants and develop joint strategies for dealing with your problems. This sort of give-and-take helps to keep you "centered," thus allowing you to maintain a reasoned approach to the task at hand.

You should find comfort in the realization that you are not alone in your efforts to resolve your credit difficulties. People in whom you can confide and with whom you can routinely discuss your financial problems can provide you with an outlet to shore up your strength.

Being Patient

Since your financial problems probably did not spring up overnight, they are not going to disappear overnight. You may have a long, hard trek ahead that will require patience and determination.

If you are faced with a staggering amount of outstanding debt, don't be discouraged by what might appear to be an insurmountable burden. Rather, be content with what you can accomplish on a day-by-day basis. As you become involved in the repayment process, take pride in your accomplishments. Soon you will see smaller debts disappear and larger debts dwindle.

Maintaining a Healthy Sense of Humor About Your Credit Problems

Be on the lookout for the lighter, more humorous aspects of the trials and tribulations of dealing with your credit problems. If you make a stupid mistake, benefit from the experience and then laugh about it. Remember, too, that tastefully delivered, discreet humor can help to soften difficult circumstances—since humor breaks down barriers and personalizes situations, consider its *careful* use as a tool for dealing with your creditors.

CHAPTER 5

The Basics of Conquering Your Debt

Changing Your Attitudes Toward Credit

If your credit problems are significant, you may have to make drastic changes in your spending habits to resolve your difficulties. This will probably mean taking a hard look at every penny you spend. You must reevaluate your standard of living, your life-style, and your current approaches to dealing with credit and financial matters. You may have to live on a budget for a couple of years.

You must be willing to accept the required changes and to make the necessary sacrifices to deal effectively with your problems. These actions are an integral part of your quest for personal financial security. The results will be well worth the sacrifices you make along the way.

Learning to Forgo Immediate Gratification

To reach your goal of paying off outstanding bills, you may have to forgo purchases that provide short-term pleasure but interfere with your longer-range goal of financial solvency.

In such instances, it's helpful to think the activity through. For example, if a dieter gorges himself, will this mean that he'll be waddling around on the beach during the summer or sensitive about his weight at an upcoming special event? Similarly, if you're dealing with credit problems, will a particular purchase force you to fall behind in your repayment activities or delay the date on which you were hoping to pay off a certain obligation? The key, obviously, is not to become distracted by the prospect of immediate gratification and never to lose sight of your long-term objective.

In the unlikely event you "fall off the wagon," don't let an isolated episode of lapsing into old spending habits destroy your long-range goal. View the episode as an aberration, and get back on the right track by refusing to succumb to future enticements.

Learning to Set Spending Priorities

You must also learn to set personal-spending priorities. Since your financial situation probably does not allow you to satisfy your every yearning, you will need to learn to make trade-offs. You may have to forgo expenses for items you might want or things you might like to do. Such sacrifices will allow you to accomplish your more important objectives.

For example, suppose you have a perfectly good winter coat but have been dreaming of a new one. You find your "dream coat" on sale at a local department store. At about the same time, your car has to be repaired at substantial expense. Since you need the car to get to and from work, paying for its repair is a priority. Your financial resources are limited and you cannot afford both purchases, so you pay for the car repairs and continue to dream about that coat. Such give-and-take teaches you to set priorities and to make the most efficient use of your available resources.

Developing Financial Goals

Many people experiencing credit difficulty have not yet learned to plan ahead by establishing financial goals. It is important that you establish financial goals in the same way you have probably already developed personal, educational, or professional goals.

By developing repayment plans with your creditors, you will be developing financial goals. Your initial goal, over a specified period of time, is to repay your creditors. Paying off your bills, repairing negative marks on your credit rating, and establishing a strong credit history are all important financial goals. A savings program, one of the most important financial goals, is crucial in meeting essential, anticipated expenses like paying college tuition, buying a car or a house, having a baby, or supporting older family members. It is also an excellent way of planning ahead for unanticipated expenses such as car repairs, a death or illness in the family, or loss of employment.

Since your financial well-being has such a tremendous impact on your life, you must plan *now* for financial matters that may arise in the future.

Eliminating Your Access to Credit

If you have, or suspect you have, a problem using credit, it is absolutely absurd to allow yourself to get further into credit difficulty or debt. By following the recommendations below, you will be protecting yourself from your worst enemy in this regard—yourself!

If you have any credit problems, under no circumstances should your debts be increased. It is crucial not to assume any new credit liability until all debts are paid and spending is brought under control. You should not carry your charge cards with you. This will eliminate your immediate access to credit. It will also make your life a lot easier if your wallet or pocketbook is stolen.

To eliminate your capacity to get further into debt, cut into quarters and return all charge cards creditors may have provided you. This will not only help you to become solvent, it will also demonstrate to creditors your good-faith efforts to discharge your current indebtedness before incurring any new obligations. If you are successful in dealing with your credit problems, most creditors will reissue your cards later. Or you can give all your charge cards to a financially responsible close friend or family member for safekeeping.

Often people argue that they should retain control of their cards so they can be used for identification purposes—for example, to cash a check. If this is your concern, retain one of your credit cards for identification purposes. Select a card that is either at or near its credit limit, thereby restricting your ability to obtain further credit.

You can also place your credit cards in a safe place in your home. While you still control the cards, the fact that you have to make an additional effort to retrieve your cards before you can use them will force you to give more thought to any future credit transactions.

If you keep your cards, you should make every effort to avoid retrieving them and incurring new debts. Should you be tempted, ask yourself the following questions:

- Why don't I pay cash?
- Is this something I absolutely have to have?
- When will I pay for this?
- What will I have to give up in exchange for this purchase?
- (If a sale item) Will the savings I reap more than offset the amount of interest I will pay on the purchase?
- Is this important enough to justify borrowing money?

After careful consideration of the above, most people will opt not to make the purchase.

If you do proceed with the purchase, remove the card from your wallet or pocketbook immediately afterward. In addition, make every effort to pay for the item as soon as possible. If you have money in your bank account, write a check and mail it to the creditor immediately. If you must wait for funds to become available, write a check and mail it as soon as you get your next paycheck.

Should you choose to retain control of your credit cards and it becomes apparent that you will continue to use them, you must either return your charge cards to your creditors or turn your credit cards over to a friend or family member. You simply must not allow yourself to continue to use credit.

Living on Cash

If you do not have enough cash to pay for an item, you probably cannot afford it through the use of credit either. As an alternative to the use of credit, try living on cash. This has the therapeutic effect of allowing you to see the immediate consequences of your spending through a direct drain on your available resources.

Counting out and handing a clerk cash for a purchase, rather than using a charge card, makes you better appreciate the gravity of your expenditure. The consequence is immediate—you see the money go from your hands to the hands of another. Credit cards do not afford the same experience, since bills are often received a month or so after a purchase is made.

If you wish to make a purchase and do not have enough cash on hand to cover it, get cash either from your bank's automatic teller machine or through cashing a check. This approach, which requires a little extra effort on your part, gives you an opportunity to reevaluate the purchase. It also forces you to witness your cash changing hands.

While writing a check does not carry the same sense of immediacy as using cash, it, too, can be therapeutic. After making a purchase by check, you should immediately deduct the amount of the check from your checkbook balance. Thus, you will see an immediate reduction in your balance as the direct result of the purchase.

By using cash or writing checks, you will be forced to make choices based on the amount of money that is available to you. If you purchase one item, you may not be able to afford something else. You have to set spending priorities.

Avoiding Bank Overdrafts

A check written on a bank account may bounce if there is not enough money in the account to cover the amount of the check. Such checks are commonly referred to in banking circles as overdrafts or NSF (for "not sufficient funds").

Several problems can result from the writing of such a "bad" check:

• You can be held criminally liable. Criminal charges are normally brought if there is evidence of a pattern of abuse (bouncing checks all over town) or if there is an apparent attempt to defraud (writing a $10,000 check on an account with an average balance of $50).

• Your name and checking account number may be given a negative rating with one of the check approval systems (like Telecheck or Chextra). This might occur if your bank or the person to whom you wrote the bad check reports it to one of these services. If this happens, you may be unable to write checks at merchants and others who participate in the check approval service. This could cause you the same type of embarrassment you might experience when a credit card charge is declined.

• The person or business to whom you wrote the check might not accept your checks in the future. This can be particularly inconvenient if the check was written for a routine payment, like rent, or embarrassing if you know the merchant.

• You might be charged a fee by a business or merchant to whom you wrote a bad check. Many establishments charge, sometimes as much as $20, as compensation for the extra effort required to collect on such a check.

• You will probably be assessed an "overdraft charge" on your bank account for a bad check. These charges normally range from $5 to $30, depending on the financial institution. Since such overdraft charges will be directly deducted from your account balance, your balance may not then be sufficient to cover other checks already written on the account. Thus, your account may be thrown so out of kilter that several checks will bounce, with overdraft charges being assessed for each. The costs of such an accumulation of overdraft charges can quickly mount up.

The key, obviously, is to not write bad checks. If you have any bad checks outstanding, you should immediately contact the persons or businesses to which they were written and arrange to make good on all such obligations. Even if you do not have enough money on hand to cover a bad check, at the least you should contact the person to whom the check was written to provide partial payment and/or a definite repayment plan to cover the obligation. If you pay cash, get a receipt. If you pay by cashier's check or money order, keep copies of all receipts.

If your account is overdrawn, or if it becomes so in the future, stop writing checks. This will help you to determine your correct balance more accurately, taking into consideration all overdraft charges assessed. It may also save you additional overdraft charges. You may need to do this for a month or so in order to see yourself clear of the problem. It may also be well worth your while either to get a current copy of your bank statement (there may be a charge) or to ask your financial institution for assistance in reconciling your account (you will probably be charged for this as well).

Until the account is sorted out, get money directly from your bank through cashing a check or using the automatic teller machine. Bills can be paid with cash (make sure to get a receipt) or by cashier's check or money order (keep copies of all receipts). It makes far better sense to spend $1.50 to $5.00 on a cashier's check or money order than to risk incurring a $30.00 overdraft charge.

Overdrafts may occur on an account for a variety of reasons—irresponsibility, mathematical errors, unavailability of deposited funds (because a "hold" was placed on a deposited item), or even intentionally. If you truly believe there are compelling reasons for the bank *not* to have assessed an overdraft charge, discuss these reasons with the bank. They might be persuaded to credit your account for all or part of the overdraft charges assessed. However, if you are responsible for such an overdraft, don't blame the bank. Accept responsibility for the problem and make every effort to assure it does not happen again. You may simply have learned your lesson the hard way.

In the future, do not write a check unless you are absolutely certain you have enough money in your account to cover it. This will mean that you will have to keep a running balance of all account activity. Make sure to record all checks written, automatic deposits, payments, service charges, fees, and automatic teller machine activities. Then, when you receive your bank statement, promptly reconcile it with your own records.

One good way of assuring you will not inadvertently overdraft is to keep a small balance in your account as a buffer. You might maintain a $100 balance in your account as a hedge against overdrafts that might result from minor mathematical errors. Pretend this $100 does not appear on your account. Maintaining a minimum balance in your account may qualify you for an account with lower or no monthly fees. If your account already requires a minimum balance, the buffer approach might save you service charges by keeping you from dipping below the required amount.

Assuming you have a good credit rating and are not over-extended, you might consider applying for a small line of credit on your bank account. Such a line of credit is frequently referred to as "overdraft protection." Essentially, the bank writes you a loan that you can then access through overdrawing your bank account up to your approved line of credit. Such a line of credit gives you flexibility by protecting you against possible overdrafts and granting you quick access to money in the event of an emergency.

The amount of the line of credit should be sufficient to cover any of your potential banking activities. However, if you are financially irresponsible in any way, you should apply for the lowest possible amount of overdraft protection. This will probably be $1,000 but will vary. By getting the smallest line of credit available, you will be limiting your potential for abuse.

You should recognize that the money represented by the line of credit is not there to use at whim, but rather is there only as a precaution or to assist you in a dire emergency. You should not view the money represented by the line of credit as a general-purpose loan. If you use it all up, it defeats your purpose in getting it in the first place. Additionally, the rate of interest on your line of credit will probably be much higher than the rate of interest you could get on a unsecured personal loan. The rate of interest on a line of credit is normally around 18 percent; the rate of interest on a personal loan will probably be closer to 13 percent.

If you trigger your line of credit, make every effort to repay the extension in full as soon as possible. Even though most of these lines of credit provide for periodic, automatic payments from your checking account balance, you should be able to make payments on your outstanding line-of-credit balance at any time. Simply request your bank either to pay off your line of credit or to make a partial payment on the outstanding balance. This will reduce the ultimate amount of interest you will have to pay for the extension. It will also restore your protection against future overdrafts. You should be aware that most institutions trigger this protection in specified increments, such as $100 at a time. Thus, you will probably need to repay whatever increment is triggered, plus interest, rather than the actual amount of the overdraft.

Developing a Realistic Budget

Understanding Your Spending Habits. As you start to develop a budget, you need to understand precisely where every penny of your spending money goes. While you may have some vague notion of how your money is spent, it is helpful to keep track of all your incidental spending.

Buy a small, pocket-size notebook, and jot down everything you spend for a week or so. Record convenience-store purchases, automobile expenses (gas, parking, tolls), meals, tips, money for coffee, soft drinks, candy, cigarettes, and so on.

You may be surprised at how much of your money goes to different types of incidental expenses per week. As a result, you may well want to reevaluate some incidental expenditures as you plan your budget.

Recommended Spending Guidelines. In addition to gaining a healthier appreciation for your incidental expenditures, you also need to understand where the bulk of your hard-earned money is going. If you are like most people, you probably do not know precisely where and how you spend your take-home pay. Thus you need to figure out carefully what percentages of your take-home pay are allocated to various types of expenditures, and to compare these expenditures with recommended spending levels.

The table below provides a handy basis for comparison of your spending habits and patterns with recommended spending guidelines. For each category simply fill in the actual amount you spend each month. Then divide this amount by your total monthly take-home pay. Multiply the answer by 100. This will give you the percentage of income you spend on each item each month.

EXAMPLE: If your monthly mortgage payment is $400, and your monthly take-home pay is $1,200, your actual housing percentage is: $400 ÷ $1,200 = .33 × 100 = 33 percent.

Category of Expenditure	Actual Amounts	Actual Percentages	Recommended Percentages
Housing (including rent or mortgage payments, condominium/ cooperative fees, utilities, supplies)	$_____	_____%	33–35%
Food	$_____	_____%	20–26%
Transportation (including gasoline/ oil, public transportation)	$_____	_____%	7–9%

Category of Expenditure	Actual Amounts	Actual Percentages	Recommended Percentages
Clothing (including dry cleaning/laundry)	$_____	_____%	6–12%
Medical (including dental, eyewear, prescriptions, health insurance premiums)	$_____	_____%	6–8%
Auto insurance	$_____	_____%	2–3%
Life insurance	$_____	_____%	2–5%
Education/advancement	$_____	_____%	2–3%
Credit obligations (including auto payments)	$_____	_____%	15–18%
Savings	$_____	_____%	2–10%
Recreation/ entertainment/child care	$_____	_____%	4–6%
Church/charities	$_____	_____%	4–10%

Compare your actual percentages with those recommended. With the exception of the savings category, higher-than-recommended percentages may indicate excessive spending and an area in which expenditures should be reevaluated or controlled. If your percentages are lower than or equal to those recommended, you fall within the recommended spending guidelines for that category.

These figures should be viewed only as guidelines. Individual circumstances will obviously vary. For example, if you are a teenage male with a bad driving record, the percentage you pay on automobile insurance will probably be considerably higher than the recommended one. Similarly, if you live in an area where housing costs are extremely high, your housing costs may necessarily consume a disproportionate share of your take-home pay.

Reducing Expenses

If you've got to do some belt tightening to get your financial affairs in order, your efforts must be built on a regime of controlling your expenses. You must place yourself in the position of controlling your costs rather than letting your expenditures control your actions. It is only through seizing the initiative, developing a game plan, and abiding by the rules you set for yourself that you will be able to deal effectively with your credit problems.

You can have a tremendous impact on expenses by finding areas where reductions can be made. For example, if housing and utilities represent a large outlay of funds each month, would alternative living arrangements—sharing a house, renting a room, or moving to a smaller apartment— be more advisable or economically feasible?

If food represents a large monthly expenditure, brown-bagging lunch at work, eating more meals at home, sharing meals with family and friends, eating out less frequently, downgrading to less expensive restaurants, shopping grocery store sales, and using coupons will help.

If transportation costs are high—auto payments, insurance premiums, parking, tolls, auto repair and maintenance—less costly modes of transportation should be considered—walking, bicycling, car and van pooling, public transportation. If you are purchasing a new vehicle, you should look for inexpensive makes and models, high fuel efficiency, and low interest rates. You should also check service records, resale values, and insurance premiums on particular vehicles prior to purchasing.

Clothing costs can be reduced by making do with last year's fashions, repairing old clothing, dressing children in hand-me-downs, and shopping sales.

Attention should also be given to telephone expenses. You

can have a substantial impact on your monthly telephone bill. Are you paying monthly leasing fees? If so, can you reduce the number of phones you have? Would buying a phone be more economical? Is there a cheaper type of local service that could satisfy your needs—local measured service and other limited forms of local service? Are you subscribing to features—custom calling, telephone answering—that you could do without (at least until bills are paid)? Have you selected a long-distance company that is tailored to your needs and calling patterns? Last but not least, don't make unnecessary long-distance calls.

Friends and family should be told you are going through a difficult time financially and should rally around to help you in your efforts to get your financial house in order. Together you should seek out inexpensive forms of recreation— bargain movie matinees, museums, art galleries, jogging, bird-watching, hunting, fishing, swimming, reading, gardening, tennis, bicycling, free concerts, picnics, walks, playing cards, dominoes, board or yard games. You'll find that you don't have to spend a lot of money to have fun.

Consider it a contest to find the best deal on a prospective purchase or the most inexpensive form of entertainment. A competition among friends or family members in trying to locate that particular model refrigerator at the lowest possible price in town can be profitable and fun. Beating the crowds to drug and department stores for advertised specials—and using coupons once you get there—can be exhilarating. You can become heady with success at finding a bottle of shampoo on the shelf that is marked fifty cents less than other similar items. You can gloat over the fact that the jar of barbecue sauce you are using cost you a fraction of its usual cost.

Increasing Income

Job Situation

If you are unable to work, you should take advantage of all governmental programs for which you qualify—unemployment compensation, workers' compensation, disability, health benefits for the unemployed, food stamps, supplemental security income, low-income energy assistance, school lunch program, Aid to Families with Dependent Children, public housing, and so on. In addition, many church and charitable organizations sponsor programs to assist low income individuals. Your local welfare office or community action program will be able to assist you in determining whether or not you are eligible for such programs.

If you are unemployed and capable of work, you should still take advantage of any of the above programs for which you qualify. However, every effort should be made to obtain gainful employment immediately. If the perfect job is not offered after the first interview, you should consider part-time or temporary employment while continuing your job search.

If you are currently employed, you should not quit your job in the hope that you will find something that will pay you more than you are making now. You should only leave your current job if a new position is a dead certainty and only after very careful analysis of the full implications of the move: Is the new job as secure as your present position? How does the compensation compare after fringe benefits (pension plans, health benefits, leave policies) and other factors (transportation costs, inconvenience) are taken into consideration? Which position holds the greatest potential for advancement, and so on?

If you are currently employed and considering an additional, part-time job to supplement your income, you should determine if this is the prudent thing to do. A part-time job should only be undertaken after a careful and thoughtful analysis of the possible repercussions. For example, moonlighting might so fatigue you that performance in your regular job might be impaired. The result could be loss of the permanent position, which could be disastrous. Similarly, would such a job take too much of your time away from family, friends, or important activities?

Paycheck

You should determine how much monthly income you actually receive. Take a hard look at your next pay stub to see what amounts are deducted from your paycheck before you get it. There are two types of payroll deductions: voluntary—life, dental, and health insurance premiums; savings deductions; charitable contributions; loan repayments; pension payments; miscellaneous; mandatory—federal, state, and local income taxes; Social Security payroll taxes, garnishment.

These payroll deductions are not as inflexible as they may at first appear. You can make decisions concerning both types of deductions that can considerably increase take-home pay.

Voluntary Deductions

Insurance. Some people have more insurance coverage than they actually need. You should reevaluate your insurance coverage to make sure you and your loved ones are adequately but not overprotected by health, dental, disability, life, automobile, homeowners', and renters' insurance.

On the other hand, do not risk reducing insurance coverage to such an extent that you and your family become underinsured.

Savings. If you have payroll savings deductions going into an account that is *earning* a rate of interest significantly less than the rate you are *paying* on current credit obligations, you might consider reducing or discontinuing savings deductions until your debts are paid. Since this may represent the disruption of a well-established savings habit, make certain to resume or increase these savings deductions once you're past your credit crisis (see section in chapter 8, "Paying Bills with Savings").

Charitable contributions. Charitable contributions are a personal decision. While such philanthropy is laudable, charitable giving might be reduced or discontinued until debts are under control. As an alternative, you might consider doing volunteer work during your spare time at your favorite charity.

Loan repayments. If you currently have loan repayments automatically deducted from your paycheck, a bill consolidation loan can reduce the amount of monthly payments withheld from your paycheck (see section in chapter 8, "Bill Consolidation Loans"). Similarly, paying off a loan can also increase take-home pay.

Miscellaneous deductions. Deductions for parking, health club memberships, and the like, may represent payments for luxuries you cannot afford with a heavy debt load. You should see if there are feasible alternatives to these expenses. For example, instead of paying for parking every month, consider public transportation or a car pool.

Mandatory Deductions

Federal and state income taxes. The federal and state income taxes that are deducted from your paycheck are based on the number of allowances you claim. Separate withholding forms for federal and state allowances must be filled out and filed with your employer. Recent federal tax reform required the filing of a new withholding statement (W-4 form) beginning January 1, 1987. If you didn't file a new W-4 by October 1, 1987, your employer was required to file one for you—designating one allowance for a single employee; two allowances for one who is married. Since the W-4 form is updated annually, you should periodically review it to see if any adjustments should be made concerning the number of allowances you claim. If the calculations on the W-4 work sheet reveal that you're overpaying your taxes, you can increase the number of allowances you are currently claiming, which will decrease the amount of money withheld from your paycheck for taxes. Conversely, if you're underpaying your taxes, you can increase the amount of tax being withheld. Completed W-4 forms should be submitted to your employer. Additionally, if you pay state income tax, a state withholding form should also be reevaluated periodically, with revised forms submitted directly to your employer. These actions could save you headaches when you file your annual income tax returns. They will also give you access to more of your monthly income (if you're overpaying) or help you avoid a big tax bill later (if you're underpaying).

Social security tax. The Social Security tax is assessed until your annual payment totals an amount prescribed by federal law. After you have reached this amount, this tax will cease to be deducted from your paycheck.

Reimbursements

Some people are lazy in seeking timely reimbursement of funds due them from different sources—personal, business, or insurance reimbursements. If you are currently strapped for cash, it just does not make sense to forgo money that may be owed to you. Don't be bashful. Assert yourself and try to collect any and all money to which you may be entitled.

You should make timely deposits into your account of any reimbursement funds you may receive. You do not want to be holding on to funds you might need in your account to cover you at the bank.

Personal Reimbursements. If you have made loans to family, friends, work colleagues, or others, ask for reimbursement. If someone is not able fully to repay an obligation, set up a repayment plan of a certain amount a month or a certain amount from each paycheck, so the repayment process can begin. You may even want to have the person who owes you money sign a repayment agreement acknowledging the debt and detailing how it will be paid (see the sample promissory note in chapter 8). If you wind up in small claims court, this agreement could serve as evidence of the debt.

If the amount is sizable, you might suggest that the person borrow money to repay you. If there has been an ongoing problem with repayment (for example, the person who owes you money has not returned your phone calls for the past six months), you can always consider pursuing repayment through small claims court. Sometimes, the threat of such action will prompt repayment. However, going to court should only be used as a last resort and may not be an option available to you if you cannot substantiate the existence of the debt.

Obviously, if you are presently in a financial bind, you should refrain from lending additional money to others.

Business Reimbursements. You should familiarize yourself with your employer's policies on employment-related expenses and seek timely reimbursement of any out-of-pocket expenses to which you may be entitled.

If you put gas in the company truck, paid parking or tolls, took clients out to lunch, or traveled out of town, and these activities were directly related to your employer's business, you should seek repayment from your employer. To this end make sure to keep track of any such expenditures by jotting notes to yourself or keeping receipts for all transactions.

You should submit for these reimbursements as soon as possible after the money has been spent on your employer's behalf. Timely submission of expense statements is important, since it may prove difficult to reconstruct events and activities months after they have taken place.

If you find that you are spending money during work-related activities that will *not* be reimbursed by your employer, ask your employer to consider extending reimbursement coverage to these expenses. If the employer refuses to reimburse, these expenses should be curtailed.

You should also familiarize yourself with your employer's "employee benefits package." These are the perks to which you may be entitled on the basis of your employment. Whenever possible, you should try to take advantage of them, whether you are entitled to reimbursement for tuition, day-care expenses, health-club membership fees, physical examinations, uniform costs, professional membership dues, annual credit card fees, and so on. In addition, if there is an expense you feel ought to be borne by your employer that is not currently covered under your employee benefits package, discuss possible reimbursement with your employer. (Be aware that some of these perks may constitute taxable income for income tax purposes.)

Insurance Reimbursements. Almost everyone has some type of insurance coverage—homeowners', renters', automobile, health, dental, accident, disability, or life. In the normal course of activities, we all need to seek reimbursement for covered expenses under some of these policies. If you are entitled to an insurance reimbursement, you should seek it in a timely fashion.

Some out-of-pocket expenditures in the form of deductibles and cost sharing, may be associated with such reimbursements. Once an annual deductible has been met, future reimbursements will not be subject to this requirement. In addition, the amount of the deductible may be considerably less than the charges for which reimbursement is being sought.

You should familiarize yourself with your insurance policies and try to maximize savings under them. Some major medical policies will reimburse at a higher rate if you take steps to reduce the overall cost of your hospital visit. For example, if you are having minor surgery, your insurance may normally reimburse approved hospital expenses at 80 percent. However, if you utilize preadmission testing—go to the hospital the day before your surgery for blood work, and so on—and spend the night before your surgery at home (rather than in the hospital), some insurance companies will reimburse your stay at 90 percent, rather than at their usual 80 percent rate.

Make certain to have copies of your insurance policies handy. Whenever possible, consult them to see if there are ways you can minimize expenses. Knowing your insurance plan provisions can also be helpful in assessing your insurance company's disposition of your claims. If a reimbursement is declined or paid at a lower level than you believe is required under your plan, appeal the decision. Write a letter to your insurance company detailing the reasons you feel reimbursement, or a higher level of reimbursement, is appropriate. Cite specific plan provisions. If your employer has an employee or health benefits officer, discuss your concerns with this person. If your insurance company refuses to alter its decision and the amount in question is substantial, you can always consult an attorney to see if legal action is appropriate.

Creating Your Budget

Once you have reevaluated your spending patterns and identified ways of maximizing your available resources, develop a realistic budget. This budget, which is based on household values and priorities, should allow for the accomplishment of financial and personal goals. It must take into consideration the needs and views of every member of your household.

Your budget should not be developed hastily; take whatever time you need to think each decision through. Keep it simple. Your budget must be practical; do not strap yourself down to a plan you cannot realistically achieve. Since you cannot possibly anticipate all your upcoming spending needs, your budget must be flexible—you must allow room for give and take. Chances are good that if you devise a three-year budget today, it may need to be adjusted to reflect changed circumstances at least a couple of times during its existence.

You should also try to reduce expenditures in every budgetary category. Many expenditures will probably have to be curtailed—by cutting back on or doing without things you have become accustomed to—until spending is brought under control and bills are paid. However, there may be little flexibility with some expenses, like mortgage or car payments. Therefore, the areas where spending reductions can be made will probably be dictated by the structure of your current expenses. After expenses have been reduced and minimal spending levels identified for each budget category, the remainder of your available funds should be earmarked for creditor payments.

If possible, budget for personal savings. Since unexpected expenses and events do occur, a meager savings plan of at least 5 percent of your take-home pay should ideally be included in your budget.

Put your budget in writing and share it with the members of your household. It is important for everyone affected to be familiar with budgetary expectations. If different members will be responsible for different expenses, identify who will be handling which budget items.

Remember, you and the members of your household are responsible for the success or failure of your budget. If you are tempted to make an unbudgeted-for expenditure, think about the impact such an expenditure will have on your spending plan. Impulse buying and unnecessary purchases must be avoided. Purchases should be made only after careful thought, planning, and consideration of their long-term repercussions.

Use the following form to create your own household budget:

Gross Income

Salary/wages	$_____
Investment income	$_____
Social Security/disability	$_____
Pensions and annuities	$_____
Alimony/child support	$_____
Unemployment	$_____
Other	$_____
Total gross income	$_____

Deductions from Gross Income

Taxes	$_____
Insurance	$_____
Savings	$_____
Other	$_____
Total deductions	$_____

AVAILABLE (NET) INCOME

Subtract applicable deductions from gross
  income $_____

EXPENSES

Housing (rent, mortgage, maintenance) $_____
Utilities $_____
Household $_____
Food $_____
Transportation $_____
Taxes (like property taxes) $_____
Insurance $_____
Children $_____
Clothing $_____
Medical $_____
Education $_____
Savings $_____
Charitable $_____
Personal $_____
Other $_____
Total expenses $_____

MONEY AVAILABLE FOR CREDITOR PAYMENTS

Subtract expenses from available income $_____

CHAPTER 6

Dealing with Your Creditors

If you are normally current on your credit obligations and suspect you may be late on a payment, it is probably a good idea to call your creditor. Explain the reasons for your tardiness, giving the date by which the creditor should expect payment. Try to make a partial payment by the due date; send the balance as soon as possible.

Assessing Your Current Debt Situation

If your credit problems are more pronounced than a simple late payment, you will probably need to assess the extent of your current indebtedness carefully, along with minimum payment and past-due amounts. *All* your debts should be taken into consideration when dealing with your credit problems, irrespective of which stage of credit difficulty you may be experiencing. You cannot be selective; you cannot pick and choose only those debts you wish to repay. On the chart below, list all your debts, providing the indicated information for each.

Name of Creditor/ Type of Account	Account Number	Minimum Payment	Past-Due Amount	Total Balance
_____	_____	$_____	$_____	$_____
_____	_____	$_____	$_____	$_____
_____	_____	$_____	$_____	$_____
_____	_____	$_____	$_____	$_____
_____	_____	$_____	$_____	$_____
_____	_____	$_____	$_____	$_____
_____	_____	$_____	$_____	$_____
_____	_____	$_____	$_____	$_____
_____	_____	$_____	$_____	$_____
_____	_____	$_____	$_____	$_____

Handling the Various Stages of Credit Difficulty

After you have listed the above information, you should next decide which stage of credit difficulty is applicable to you. Depending on the extent of your current indebtedness, you will need to respond to your stage of credit difficulty by taking the prescribed actions for dealing with your creditors.

Early Stages

The early stages of credit difficulty are marked by being routinely late on payments, paying penalties, being over approved credit limits, and being a month or more behind on obligations. It may be relatively easy to rectify the problem by simply cutting back on spending for a couple of months and getting caught up on bills.

If you find yourself in the early stages of credit difficulty, contact your creditors immediately. Explain the reasons for your current bind and give assurances (with dates if possible) of your intent to pay. Your creditors will probably be very willing to help you develop a temporary, revised payment plan, since you have recognized a problem and are taking steps to correct it before it gets too large. As you pay your bills, make the minimum payments as they become due. Failure to make timely payments could damage your credit rating.

Later Stages

If your problem has progressed into the later stages of credit difficulty, your task will be more difficult. Bills may be months overdue, minimum payments may be totally out of reach, and creditors may be contacting you.

You should seize the initiative by contacting your creditors immediately. Grabbing the bull by the horns—by voluntarily contacting your creditors—may keep creditors from taking further action or initiating collection activities against you. You are seizing the initiative at a time when you probably still have many options available to you. Remember, it is much easier to deal with a creditor in the earlier stages, since options tend to diminish as the quality of the dialogue between creditor and debtor deteriorates. Once a line of communication has been established, make every effort to keep it open.

Since dealing with creditors who are engaged in collection activities can sometimes be difficult, many people are tempted to avoid such collection activities (by refusing to return phone calls, pretending they are not the debtor when a creditor calls, or generally failing to be responsive to the creditor's overtures). However, absolutely the worst thing you can do if you are experiencing credit difficulty is to avoid your creditors. There is no way you are going to be able to wish the problem away. If you don't talk to your creditors now, you will more than likely talk to them later, perhaps in court. The preferable, responsible approach is to deal with your creditors.

If you believe any of the collection activities that are being used against you are unfair or abusive, consult the section on "Bill Collectors" in chapter 7 for a discussion of your rights under the federal Fair Debt Collection Practices Act.

When contacting your creditors, you will need to negotiate repayment plans, based on the recommendations provided in the section that follows.

Final Stages

During the final stages of credit difficulty, court proceedings may be threatened or pending against you, your wages may be subject to garnishment, goods may have been attached, and articles repossessed. (To familiarize yourself with the permissible actions creditors may take against you to collect a debt, and your rights concerning each type of activity, please consult chapter 7.)

After months of neglect in repaying accounts and refusals to deal with creditors when they attempted to contact you, you may think it impossible to see yourself clear of your current credit difficulties. Even if you have been conscientiously trying to handle your credit obligations, your condition may have so deteriorated that your repayment efforts have barely scratched the surface of your total indebtedness. Indeed, you may believe your credit difficulties have progressed beyond your ability to effectively deal with them.

Consumer Credit Counseling Services

Low-cost, professional help in dealing with credit problems is available through Consumer Credit Counseling Services (CCCS) located throughout the country. CCCS has provided reasonably priced, badly needed assistance to thousands of debtors. These nonprofit organizations are staffed by professional financial counselors who will give you sound advice on your credit problems. The cost of CCCS is minimal, with a small, voluntary monthly contribution normally requested. The bulk of CCCS funding comes from local creditors who subsidize their activities.

If you choose to enter a CCCS program, they will help you set up a budget and develop a realistic repayment plan. CCCS will also contact creditors on your behalf to negotiate a repayment schedule (the same types of activities recommended in the section which follows). CCCS's direct contact with creditors is oftentimes crucial since they serve as an intermediary between you and your creditors, where relationships may be strained. If creditors are contacting you, CCCS can serve as a buffer. After you have set up a CCCS appointment, simply tell your creditors you are seeking professional assistance in dealing with your credit problems through CCCS. The creditor can then contact CCCS to confirm the existence of your appointment. Involvement in the CCCS program not only establishes a repayment mechanism but it also demonstrates to creditors a good-faith effort to solve your financial problems.

While individual circumstances will obviously vary, a typical CCCS program is a two- to three-year repayment plan during which your outstanding debts will be repaid. As part of your plan, you will be required to:

- Not incur any new debt until your repayment plan has been completed
- Make payments directly to CCCS once a month, either by cashier's check or money order

Once CCCS has established a repayment plan that is acceptable to both you and your creditors, they will, on receiving your monthly payments, mail checks directly to your creditors.

If you participate in the CCCS program, it is *extremely* important that you make the required monthly payments to CCCS in a timely fashion. For many creditors, CCCS may represent their last straw in dealing with you. If you fail to live up to your obligations under the CCCS repayment plan, creditors may feel their only remaining alternative is to pursue legal action against you.

For the location of the CCCS office nearest you, please consult appendix 2, your local telephone directory, or library. In addition, individual creditors, your local Chamber of Commerce, Better Business Bureau, or Retail Merchants Association (if your community has one) should be able to direct you to the CCCS office that serves your area. This information can also be obtained from:

National Foundation for Consumer Credit
8701 Georgia Avenue, Suite 507
Silver Spring, MD 20910
(301) 589-5600

Developing Repayment Plans with Your Creditors

You must make repayment arrangements or develop repayment plans with all creditors. When contacting your creditors, be forthcoming with them. Provide each creditor with enough information about your financial situation and any extenuating circumstances so they feel confident there is some basis on which you should be granted special consideration.

Creditor payments must be determined on a pro rata basis. Hence your payment to a particular creditor must bear some relation to the size of your debt with that creditor, contrasted with your other obligations. Smaller debts will result in smaller payments; larger debts will yield larger payments. When negotiating repayment plans with creditors, stress that you are treating all creditors fairly through the development of a pro rata repayment plan. Let creditors know that any attempt to satisfy the demands of a single creditor, through disproportionate payments, may be detrimental to your other creditors. Do not pay any one creditor to the exclusion of others.

Assure each creditor that you do not intend to create any new obligations until all accounts are paid or at least brought under control. Be realistic when developing repayment plans with creditors, making certain you can maintain the agreed-on payments. Failure to abide by the terms of your repayment plan could be disastrous. Once a repayment plan has been devised, make every effort to follow this agreement tenaciously.

Restructuring Obligations

After you have established a repayment plan with a creditor, you must have your account records corrected to reflect the revised payment terms. This will essentially "clean up" the creditor's file on your account, and most importantly, the way your account is transmitted to credit reporting agencies.

After you have followed the steps outlined above for developing repayment plans with creditors, make certain each creditor has:

- Corrected all past due balance amounts, which should now be zero
- Revised the minimum payment due to reflect your new monthly payments under the new payment schedule

Since creditors often fail to make these corrections on their own, either check your monthly statement or call your creditor to make sure both of these matters have been taken care of. If they have not, urge your creditor to make the needed corrections immediately. Sometimes creditors are reluctant to make these changes and might require a little coaxing. If the creditor is particularly intransigent, suggest that the figures be revised after you have demonstrated a commitment to repaying the obligation (that is, after you've made payments under the new plan for three months). Then, if the creditor agrees to such a proposal, make prompt monthly payments, call back after the prescribed period has elapsed, and renew your request to have these figures adjusted.

By accomplishing this type of restructuring, you will not only be repaying the obligation, but also redeeming yourself for credit rating purposes. For instance, assume your account was six months past due. Your creditor has now removed all past due balances, and has established a new minimum payment. If you make regular payments under your new payment plan, your credit report will reflect that you are currently making payments within thirty days, or according to the terms of your (new) agreement.

On the other hand, if new minimum payment amounts are not reflected, and past due balances are still reported, you might be paying the same amount of money to the creditor each month. But, the account may still be reflected on your credit report as being months past due. The follow-ing example illustrates this point:

Before contacting your creditor about a repayment plan. Your original agreement required $100 monthly payments, you had made no payments for six months, your outstand-ing account balance was $700, your minimum payment was $600, and your past-due amount was $500.

After contacting your creditor, negotiating a repayment plan, and revising the minimum-payment and past-due amounts. Your new monthly payments are $50, your out-standing account balance is still $700, your new minimum payment is $50, and your new past-due amount is $0.

If the creditor fails to revise the minimum-payment and past-due amounts, after your first month's payment under your new payment plan, your new monthly payments are $50, your balance, excluding new interest charges, is $650, your minimum payment is $650, and your past-due amount is $550.

Refinancing Obligations

It may be possible to refinance some obligations if you have several different accounts with one creditor. For example, assume you have the following outstanding balances on three accounts at your local bank:

Checking account line of credit	$2,000 or 18%
Credit card line of credit	$2,000 or 21%
Personal loan	$1,000 or 17.5%

Also, assume you are behind on your payments for every one of these obligations; the minimum payments are beyond your reach. Ask your banker to refinance your obligations—

to write you a new loan for the specific purpose of closing and paying your delinquent accounts with the bank.

Consolidating these outstanding obligations into a single loan will result in one monthly payment. Since this new loan may stretch repayment over a period of two to three years, payments will probably be more manageable. You may also benefit from a lower interest rate, if the interest rate on the new loan is lower than you were paying on your old obligations. However, if the interest rate will increase under the new loan, it may not be the loan for you.

When approaching your banker, stress that you are not asking the bank to lend you any more money. You are asking for a realignment of your current obligations, nothing more. All you want is a "second chance." Bear in mind that if the new loan is at a lower interest rate than you are being assessed on your current obligations, the bank will probably end up earning less than they would have under your original payment plans.

Writing Off Obligations

If one of your accounts has been a continuing problem for a creditor to collect, you might be able to benefit from a write-off. Rather than spending more money on collection activities against you, the creditor might be willing to accept something less than full payment to simply get rid of the account. Some creditors may write off a debt by acceptance of a partial payment as payment in full. Often this figure will be the amount of the principal due on the account, with the creditor forgiving accrued, unpaid interest charges. Creditors are under no obligation to write off an account. Those willing to negotiate write-offs do so as a matter of sheer economics.

You should never attempt a write-off if, by paying the

write-off creditor, you will be unable to pay or will fall behind in your payments to other creditors. You must also have the money, in hand, to pay the write-off amount. Partial payments are normally not accepted; time deadlines are usually imposed.

If you meet the above requirements, contact your creditor to request that a particular account be handled as a write-off. Since the fate of this proposal will be determined by the credit supervisor, do not expect an immediate answer. Someone should contact you regarding your request. If you do not hear from the creditor within a reasonable time (that is, within a week), call back and ask to discuss the matter with the credit supervisor directly. If a write-off is approved, a figure will be proposed. Before accepting such a proposal, determine whether or not the particular account is reflected on your credit report.

If the account does *not* currently appear on your credit report, you might proceed with the write-off payment. However, this write-off account may later appear on your credit report if the creditor starts submitting its accounts to a credit reporting agency. If the account currently appears on your credit report, or if you fear it will appear in the future, you should negotiate with the creditor as to how the account will be reported. If the creditor is willing to report the account as current, rather than as a write-off, you can proceed with the payment. However, if the account will be reported as a write-off on your credit report, do *not* pursue the write-off. Instead, try to restructure the account with the creditor.

General Recommendations

Be pragmatic when approaching creditors about developing repayment plans, restructuring, refinancing or writing off obligations. Listen to what they say, and try to determine their bottom line. Be creative in your approach. If you can get the creditor to move a step or two in your direction, accept what you can get for the time being. Wait a couple of months, then see if you can move them a little closer to your goal.

You will need to speak with the credit manager. The clerk who answers the phone will *not* have the authority to make the adjustments you are requesting. You may find cold water being tossed on your proposal, and you may be told that this sort of approach is not part of the creditor's established procedures. Be courteous yet persistent.

If you get someone on the phone who refuses even to consider your proposal, call back the next day or during the lunch hour, to see if you can talk with someone more responsive. If the first person you speak with declines your proposal, politely ask to speak with the supervisor. Make sure to record the names and positions of everyone you speak with. If you keep running into brick walls, ask to speak with the head of the collections or customer service department.

This may get sticky if the creditor takes a hard-line approach and reasons, "Why should I accommodate some derelict who is behind on his bills?" In response, you should tell the creditor:

1. You are making a conscientious effort to develop a reasonable repayment plan.
2. Under such a plan, you will be able to make timely payments which may save the creditor time and money through the cessation of collection activities on your account.

Your proposal will require some extra effort on the part of the creditor. You should, therefore, bend over backward to let them know how appreciative you are of their efforts.

CHAPTER 7

Creditors' Remedies and Your Rights

If you have ever been late on or missed a payment to one of your creditors, you have probably been exposed to some creditor collection tactics. If you have ever defaulted on an obligation, you no doubt felt the brunt of the creditor's efforts to collect the debt you owed. But how far can a creditor go when attempting to collect a debt? What are your rights? How are you protected against overzealous creditors and their collection techniques?

Creditors have various collection devices at their disposal when seeking repayment of debts owed to them. Normally, the severity of their collection efforts bears a direct correlation to the difficulties they encounter when attempting to collect a debt. For example, if a creditor has had to track your movements across the country, or you consistently refuse to discuss your indebtedness, you may be subjected to fairly severe collection activities. These could include court proceedings and, if the creditor obtains a judgment against you, legal writs enforcing the judgment.

So, if you are delinquent on any obligations to creditors, you must strive to resolve repayment problems as quickly as possible by immediately contacting your creditors. You must seize the opportunity to pay up voluntarily, before your account is referred to an outside collection agency or legal proceedings are brought against you. If you contact your creditors during the early stages of their collection efforts, you will probably have more repayment options available to you. You might also be able to reduce your ultimate costs, which could increase because of late payment charges, over-the-limit fees, interest expenses, attorneys' fees, collection costs, court costs, and the like. In addition, early resolution of the problem could minimize damage to your credit report.

From the outset, understand that creditors don't enjoy collection activities any more than you do. In fact, collection activities cost creditors millions of dollars a year. However, the fact remains that if you legitimately owe a debt to a creditor, the creditor has the legal right to take permissible actions to recover the amount of your indebtedness. And the chances are pretty good that your creditor will use whatever means required.

Informal Collection Activities

If you are a little late on a payment, your creditor will probably send you a gentle reminder that your payment is past due: "We know it's easy to forget, but we don't have your money yet." Or your next statement might note, "Our records indicate your account is now past due." Such notices are designed to coax your payment along.

If these tactics fail to produce a payment on your account, the next communications will probably be a little more urgent and belligerent in their tone: "Your account is now two months past due. Please remit immediately." Similarly, you may receive a letter stating, "To avoid further collection activities on this account, please contact us immediately." Or,

"Your account has been turned over to a collection agency for repayment." Often such "dunning notices" will come as mailgrams, conveying a sense of urgency about repayment.

Should the above tactics fail to prompt a payment, your creditor may temporarily suspend the account or freeze your line of credit (not allow any new charges) until the past-due amount is paid and the account returns to a current status. In such cases, your creditor may ask you to "leave home without it," by demanding that you return your credit cards or stop using the problem account. Sometimes, after a period of nonpayment, creditors will simply close your account.

Since specific creditor rights concerning the collection of your account will be included in your original loan agreement, carefully read that agreement to determine your creditor's rights. For example, default clauses, which define precisely what constitutes a default by the debtor, are found in most consumer contracts. Many consumer credit contracts also contain acceleration clauses, which allow a creditor to terminate your account and to demand immediate payment in full of the outstanding balance because of late payments or failure to make payments as required under your agreement. Often loan agreements will contain language making you liable for any attorneys' fees, collection costs, court costs, or other costs the creditor may incur while attempting to collect on your account.

In addition to creditor rights that may be spelled out in consumer credit contracts, the law may entitle creditors to additional rights. For example, if you default on a loan repayment to a bank, the bank has a right to extinguish your account. In most states, such a right can be enforced without your consent and without a court order.

If you are behind in your payments to a creditor, do not attempt to use the account until your payment situation has been corrected. This could save you the embarrassment of having a credit card transaction declined or a credit card seized when you attempt to use it. In addition, further attempts to use your delinquent account will only exacerbate problems with your creditor.

Creditor Prohibitions

Creditors are prohibited from engaging in certain types of activities, such as including unconscionable provisions in consumer credit contracts. In consumer credit contracts:

• You cannot be required to give up your right to be notified of court proceedings against you should the creditor sue you on the obligation. Formerly, "confessions of judgment," under which a debtor signed an agreement admitting to the debt and waiving the right to receive court papers should a lawsuit be initiated, were commonplace. Confessions of judgment are no longer allowed.

• You cannot be required to give up protections afforded under state law, which allow you to keep certain personal belongings, nor can you be required to use specified household items or objects with sentimental value as security for a debt. However, if the creditor financed your purchase of the item and it was used as security for the debt, the creditor is free to repossess the item.

In addition, if you agree to wage deductions for the payment of an obligation, you must retain the right to cancel such deductions at any time. Creditors can charge you late fees if you do not make your required payments on time, but they cannot assess a late fee for your failure to pay other late fees.

The above prohibitions are required by credit practices rules adopted by the federal regulatory agencies that supervise creditor activities.

Bill Collectors

Distinguishing Between Different Types of Bill Collectors

If bill collectors are attempting to contact you, you must be able to distinguish between the two different types of bill collectors, primary and third party.

Primary Bill Collectors. A primary bill collector attempts to collect a debt owed directly by the purchaser to an individual or firm—merchant, retailer, or supplier. Examples of primary bill collectors include in-house collections activities by credit card companies, department stores, hospitals, building contractors, and so on. Their efforts are in-house attempts to collect debts directly owed to a creditor.

Third-Party Bill Collectors. Most creditors will attempt to recover money owed them through their own, in-house collection activities. However, should in-house collection activities fail to produce timely repayment of an obligation, creditors may refer their accounts to a third-party bill collector. Third-party bill collectors are, in essence, hired guns who are authorized to collect debts owed to their client (someone other than the third-party bill collector). There are two types of third-party bill collectors:

1. Collection agencies
2. Law firms that routinely act as collection agents

Credit Report Implications

If you are currently dealing with an in-house bill collector, it is in your best interest to resolve any payment problems with your creditor directly. Since your account is still being handled by your original creditor, you may not yet have caused irreparable damage to your credit rating. Through a repayment plan, you may be able to minimize any negative submissions on your credit report.

However, if your account is or has been referred to a third-party bill collector, it will probably be reflected on your credit report as having been placed for collection. A negative mark on your credit rating may be difficult, if not impossible, to remove from your credit report. Therefore, if it is not already too late, try to deal with your credit obligations before a third-party bill collector becomes involved.

Your Rights Concerning Bill Collectors' Activities

The federal Fair Debt Collection Practices Act (FDCPA) provides debtor protection against abusive, unfair, and unreasonable collection activities. While the protections of the act *do not* extend to the activities of primary bill collectors (that is, in-house collection activities), many primary bill collectors try to conform their activities to those permissible under the act. The act *does* apply to collection activities engaged in by both types of third-party bill collectors.

Under the Fair Debt Collection Practices Act, third-party bill collectors must not engage in unreasonable collection activities. These protections extend not only to the debtor but also to his or her spouse, parents (if the debtor is a minor), guardian, executor, or administrator. The act limits them in the following ways:

Finding Your Location.   If a bill collector knows you are represented by an attorney, the collector's communication must be limited to your attorney. Unless your attorney fails to respond, the collector cannot contact you or anyone else.

If you are not represented by an attorney, a bill collector is allowed to talk with others only to the extent necessary to determine your whereabouts. Normally, collectors cannot contact someone more than once concerning your whereabouts. When communicating with others, they must identify themselves and indicate that they are simply confirming or correcting information about your location. "Your location" is defined as information concerning your residence, home phone number, and place of employment. Location information does *not* include work phone numbers; names and phone numbers of supervisors; salaries or dates of paydays. Only if specifically asked are bill collectors allowed to reveal the identity of their employer.

Communicating with You. A bill collector may contact you in person, by mail, telephone, or telegram. However, all communications with you must occur at times and places convenient to you. Unless you have communicated special circumstances to the bill collector (for example, you work at night and sleep during the day) and agreed to allow the creditor to contact you at unusual times of the day, reasonable times are considered to extend from 8:00 A.M. until 9:00 P.M. local time at *your* location, seven days a week. If a bill collector has credible information indicating specific times that are inconvenient for you (as in the example above), such times are off limits. A bill collector cannot contact you while you are at the dentist, buying groceries, at the day-care center, working out at the gym, and so on. You also cannot be contacted at your place of employment if your employer prohibits such communications.

You may notify the collector in writing that you refuse to pay the debt or that you want the collector to stop further communications with you. In such instances, the collector can only contact you again to notify you that further collection activities are being terminated, that certain remedies available to them may be enforced, or that a specified remedy will be pursued.

Communicating with Others. Except for obtaining information concerning your whereabouts, a bill collector cannot communicate with any third parties concerning the collection of your debt unless you give your consent or a court order permits such communications. Thus, a bill collector cannot tell anyone that you owe any debt. This means the collector cannot discuss the debt with your boss, tell the receptionist, leave a message about the debt with your apartment manager, post a sign on your front door, or otherwise discuss your indebtedness with anyone else in any fashion.

Protection from Harassment or Abuse. A debt collector cannot harass, oppress, or abuse you or anyone else concerning the collection of a debt. For example, you are protected against

- Threats or implied threats of violence or use of harm to any person, reputation, or property
- Use of obscene, profane, or abusive language (including religious slurs, racial or sexual epithets, calling the debtor names)
- Publication of lists of debtors (except to credit bureaus)
- Advertisement for sale of any debt
- Abusive, annoying, or harassing activities with the telephone (including repeated or continuous telephone calls or the caller's failure to identify him- or herself when calling) or when otherwise contacting the consumer or third parties

Protection from False, Deceptive, or Misleading Representations. A bill collector is prohibited from using false, deceptive, or misleading representations concerning the collection of a debt. Bill collectors are prohibited from:

• Using symbols in correspondence that represent or intimate that the debt collector is in any way associated with the United States or any state government.

• Using any documents designed falsely to imply that they are government documents or court papers or otherwise misrepresent authorship of documents.

• Falsely representing or implying that documents are *not* court papers or do not require consumer attention.

• Falsely representing or implying that they are attorneys.

• Falsely representing the character, amount, or legal status of any debt.

• Falsely representing or implying that nonpayment will result in the arrest or imprisonment of any person, or that they will garnish, attach, or sell property or wages of any person, unless they intend to do so and it is legal.

• Threatening to take actions that are not intended or that are not legally permissible (for example, bill collectors cannot threaten criminal action unless they actually intend to pursue such an action; nor can they threaten to attach your tax refund since this cannot be legally accomplished). Similarly, debt collectors cannot falsely threaten other types of actions (such as reporting the debt to credit bureaus or assessing penalties or other charges if the debt is not paid) unless they have the legal right to pursue such options. In addition, debt collectors cannot threaten to contact an employer or other parties about your debt since they are prohibited by law from engaging in such activities.

• Falsely representing or implying that a transfer of the debt will cause the consumer to lose any claim or defense, or become subject to any practice prohibited by the federal Fair Debt Collection Practices Act.

• Falsely representing or implying that you committed any crime (such as fraud or similar offenses).

• Communicating or threatening to communicate false credit information (such as failing to indicate the status of disputed information on your credit report).

• Using false representations or deceptive means concerning debt collection or to obtain information about the consumer.

• Falsely representing or implying that an account has been turned over to innocent purchasers for value.

• Using any business, company, or organization name other than the collector's true name.

• Falsely representing or implying that they operate or work for a credit-reporting agency.

Protection from Unfair or Unconscionable Practices.   Debt collectors are prohibited from using unfair or unconscionable debt collection practices. Examples of prohibited unfair or unconscionable debt collection practices include:

• Collecting any amount greater than your debt, unless the amount is expressly authorized by your loan agreement (including collection, interest, service, or returned check charges, or late-payment fees) or is permitted by law

• Accepting a check postdated (made out for a future date) by more than five days unless timely written notice of deposit is made to you prior to deposit

• Soliciting any postdated check for purposes of threatening or instituting criminal prosecution

• Depositing a postdated check prior to the date on the check

• Causing you to incur telephone (including collect calls) or telegram charges by concealing the purpose of their communications

- Sending you postcards, using see-through envelopes, or using any language or sign on an envelope or telegram that in any way indicates the existence of a debt or their collection activities; or
- Sending you an "in care of" letter unless you live at, or accept mail at, the other party's address

Other Bill Collector Prohibitions. If you make a payment to a collection agency that is handling several of your accounts, debt collectors cannot apply your payment to any debt with which you disagree (disputed debts). Rather, debt collectors must apply your payment to the debt(s) you choose.

In addition, should you be taken to court by a debt collector, you have the right to be sued in a convenient forum. This means that the collectors can only sue you in one of the following locations:

- Where you reside
- Where the contract giving rise to the debt was signed
- Where the property is located (if an interest in real property is involved and the property secures the debt)

However, if a bill collector obtains an initial judgment observing the above convenient-forum limitations, the collector is then free to enforce such a judgment and pursue judicial collection remedies in another jurisdiction.

What Is a Debt Collector Required to Do? Your bill collector has the following affirmative obligations concerning the collection of your account. When communicating with you about your debt, a bill collector is required to disclose clearly that he or she is attempting to collect a debt and that any information obtained will be used for debt collection purposes. Also, if the bill collector does not provide you with the information listed below during the first contact with you, it must be disclosed in writing within five days of the first contact:

- Amount of the debt being collected
- Identity of the creditor to whom you owe the money
- That the collector will assume the debt's validity unless you dispute it within thirty days
- How you can contest the validity of the debt

If you contest the validity of the debt in writing within thirty days of the bill collector's initial contact with you, the bill collector cannot contact you again without written proof of the debt (that is, copies of a judgment, sales slips, statements, and the like). However, the bill collector is free to proceed with collection activities until the time your dispute is received. In addition, your failure to dispute the accuracy of a debt on receipt of the above notice *cannot* be used by a court as an admission of your liability on the debt.

The foregoing pages describe your rights under the federal Fair Debt Collection Practices Act. However, your state may have its own debt collection law, which may afford you additional protections. Such state-provided protections are permissible so long as they are not inconsistent with federal law. To see if you are entitled to more than the minimum protections provided by federal law, check your state law.

Court Proceedings

You must make every effort to keep a court judgment from being issued against you. If a creditor threatens to take you to court over a debt, try to come to some accommodation before a court appearance is required. If legal proceedings have been initiated against you, try to resolve the matter so the case can be dropped or dismissed before a judgment is issued.

If you actually find yourself in court, make certain to assert all defenses you can substantiate. For example, if you contest the amount of the debt, make your position known. Bring along any documentation (like prior statements or canceled checks) that you may have substantiating the amount you allege.

If the validity of the debt is not in question, see if the judge and your creditor will agree to a repayment plan as a temporary solution, instead of a final judgment favoring your creditor. If an acceptable repayment plan can be devised, ask the court to stay (or delay) the effective date of the judgment to allow you to make payments under the plan. Then, after you have made the required payments in a timely fashion, petition the court to dismiss the case against you since your obligation to the creditor has been satisfied.

One of the best ways of avoiding court proceedings is to develop a repayment plan with your creditors (see chapter 6). After you have developed a reasonable repayment plan with your creditors (determined on a pro rata basis) and are conscientiously making payments according to your plan, most creditors will be hard pressed to drag you into court, since the creditor has some reasonable expectation of payment. Lawsuits consume valuable court time, hence a judge is unlikely to view favorably a creditor's lawsuit on an obligation that is already in the process of being repaid.

Should your creditors seem intent on taking you to court, assure them you will make your current repayment efforts known to the court. In addition, let your creditors know you have no intention of paying them to the exclusion of others. Tell them that you're attempting to accommodate all your creditors through the development of a fair and equitable repayment plan. Advise them that if they take you to court on the debt you owe them, you will be forced to notify your other creditors so they can protect their repayment interests in the same lawsuit.

If the creditor still insists upon dragging you to court, be prepared to defend your repayment plan, providing a copy of it, along with documentation of your available resources, your ongoing payments to all other creditors, and your indebtedness with each creditor. Obviously, the above approach is predicated on a reasonable repayment plan. You cannot make token payments to your creditors and expect such payments to serve as a defense. Rather, you must be able to demonstrate that you are making every effort, given your current financial circumstances, to repay your obligations to the best of your ability.

Should you receive a summons to appear in court concerning one of your obligations, go to court and enter an appearance on the date and at the time designated on the summons. Under no circumstances should you simply fail to appear for your scheduled court appearance. If you don't show up, your interests will never be represented before the court and your creditor may be granted a default judgment, which might be enforced through garnishment of your wages, attachment of your property, or other legal remedies (see discussion below). Should you later try to contest this default judgment, you will have to petition the court to reopen your case and will be charged with the burden of disproving the court's earlier findings.

If you absolutely cannot make it to court on the appointed day, call the court clerk and ask for an extension or an alternate date that is more convenient to your schedule. Most court rules allow for a limited number of schedule changes. However, since these vary with each court, check with the clerk to see how many continuances you may be allowed. If you are granted a continuance, make every effort to resolve the conflict with your creditor before your rescheduled court date. Or, if you plan to use a repayment plan as a defense, keep current in your payments (since the delay will give you extra time to make additional payments under your repayment plan). In addition, if you are actively negotiating with your creditor concerning repayment of the obligation, you may jointly ask for an extension of time to hammer out an acceptable payment plan.

Though appearing as a defendant in a legal proceeding can be a very intimidating experience, don't despair. If you can afford one, hire an attorney to represent you. If there is a law school in your area, contact it to see if free or low-cost legal advice is available. Similarly, if low-income legal services are available in your area and you qualify, get assistance from them. You might even be surprised to learn that many courts utilize law students, retired people, or volunteers who attempt to negotiate settlements before the case ever goes before the judge. If you're particularly scared, you might consider dropping in on your designated court's proceedings a few days before your scheduled appearance date to witness how cases are handled. Or take a friend or loved one along with you to court for support. Remember, the only way you can be assured your interests are represented is to make an appearance on your court date.

If a judgment should be rendered against you, it will be recorded in the court's records. Court record judgments are likely to appear on your credit report. Since it was a judicial act that created the judgment, the only way a judgment can be removed from your credit report is by your petitioning the court to vacate its judgment through another judicial act. This can be extremely difficult; it is far preferable to try to avoid getting such a judgment rendered against you in the first place.

Liens

Sometimes creditors can develop an interest in, a right to possess, or a claim against your property (both real and personal). Such an interest, which is legally recognized, is called a lien. In essence, a lien is an encumbrance on your property that must be satisfied before your property or the proceeds from the sale of your property can be used for other purposes. Thus, your creditor can develop a secured or protected interest in specific property you own. This lien may give your creditor priority over the claims of others.

If several liens are placed on the same piece of property, state law will usually control the order in which they will be satisfied. Normally liens will be ranked according to the order in which they were created. Under this "first in time" approach, a secured creditor's interest will take precedence over any other interests (including those of subsequent creditors) that might later be created. Thus a creditor holding your first mortgage will have his claims satisfied before any subsequent lienholders. If the value of the property is sufficient fully to satisfy the first lienholder, surplus funds will then be available for other lienholders, general creditors (those who do not hold liens), and then the debtor. If the value of the property doesn't satisfy a particular creditor's lien, the lienholder will be entitled to all available funds and will then become a general creditor for the remaining unpaid balance.

Consensual Liens.   A consensual lien is created if you borrow money to purchase property and your promise to repay uses the property as collateral for the loan. By allowing the property to be used as collateral, you are also specifically consenting to the creation of a lien against the property to protect the creditor. Thus, if you take out a home loan, second mortgage, or home improvement or home equity loan, you are creating a consensual lien against your home. Other types of consensual liens are also commonplace: car loans, appliance or furniture purchases, and so on.

Statutory Liens.   Statutory liens arise through the operation of law. Even though the debtor has not specifically given consent for the creation of a lien, the law recognizes certain circumstances where liens automatically arise. Examples include: tax and landlords', artisans', and mechanics' liens. Thus if you have your car repaired and do not pay the mechanic, the law implies a mechanic's lien against your car for the value of the repairs.

Judicial Liens.   Judicial liens can arise from either prejudgment or postjudgment collection efforts by your creditor. For example, a prejudgment lien will be created if the court allows your creditor to attach your property while a lawsuit against you is pending (that is, a lien will be placed on your property). A postjudgment lien might be created if your creditor garnishes your wages (that is, your creditor places a lien on your wages until a judgment is satisfied). The judicial remedies discussed below, if successful, will oftentimes result in the placement of judicial liens to secure payment of the judgment.

Judicial Remedies

Creditors have various remedies at their disposal to secure judicial repayment of your debt. While you cannot be sent to jail for nonpayment of your debts (debtors' prisons don't exist), judicial remedies, which forcibly extract payments of money or articles of value from recalcitrant debtors, can be quite burdensome and inconvenient. Some of these are prejudgment remedies (which allow for the protection of the creditor's interests while a court proceeding is taking place and before a final judgment has been rendered). Others are postjudgment remedies (available only after a final judgment has been rendered against you).

Although these remedies, which are usually governed by state law, do not vary greatly from state to state, the procedures creditors may use to accomplish them do vary. The effective periods for these remedies also vary by state. For these reasons consult your state's laws to determine whether your creditor is proceeding against you in accordance with local law.

While your creditor's actions will probably be bound by your state's laws, a general discussion of the basic characteristics of various creditor remedies is helpful.

Attachment of Property.   Attachment is a prejudgment remedy that creates a creditor's temporary, provisional interest in property you possess. This right is nonpossessory while the lawsuit is being litigated. You always retain possession of the property. If your creditor wins the lawsuit against you, an attachment ripens into a full lien. If you win the lawsuit, the attachment dissolves.

Attachment is a remedy *seldom* available to creditors. Courts will normally only grant motions for attachment if the creditor is likely to have difficulty recovering payment of the judgment from you.

Replevin.   Replevin is another provisional, prejudgment remedy. In a replevin action, someone may sue you to recover possession of specific goods you possess in which they claim an interest and to which they allege an immediate right to possession. If the court grants a replevin motion, you may be required immediately to deliver the property in question to the other party. While possession will change, the question of who retains title or who has the ultimate right to possession will be resolved by the outcome of the lawsuit.

Property Garnishment. Property garnishment can be either a pre- or postjudgment remedy available to creditors. In a property garnishment action, your property is not in your own possession but in the hands of a third party. Property garnishment does not arise automatically but occurs only through the filing of a garnishment motion by your creditor.

If a court orders a garnishment against you, your bank or any other holder of your property will be instructed to either hold your property (for example, funds in your bank account) being garnished or deliver it to the court. If a prejudgment remedy is pursued, your property will be held until the lawsuit between you and your creditor has been resolved. Thus, a provisional lien is created, which is contingent on your creditor winning the lawsuit. If your creditor wins, your bank or any other holder of your property will be directed to withhold your property from you and distribute it instead to your creditor. Your access to the property will be restored once your judgment has been paid. On the other hand, if you win the lawsuit, your property will either be released from the garnishment or returned to you.

If a postjudgment garnishment is used, your creditor will use garnishment as a means of executing his judgment against you. Thus, if you fail to pay a creditor's outstanding judgment, he or she may garnish funds in your bank account or garnish your wages (see below) in order to satisfy the judgment.

Wage Garnishment. A wage garnishment is a remedy available to a creditor legally to obtain a percentage of your compensation to satisfy an outstanding judgment. Wage garnishment is a postjudgment remedy and only occurs after a court of competent jurisdiction has issued a final judgment. Thus, a wage garnishment will not miraculously appear overnight, without notice. Rather, it represents the culmination of a series of judicial events that should put you on notice that a garnishment might occur.

Specific restrictions on wage garnishments have been enacted by the U.S. Congress to: (1) exempt wage earners from burdensome garnishments, (2) protect employment of wage earners, and (3) prevent bankruptcies. Garnishment protection applies only to compensation currently payable or to become payable to you in the future. Thus, compensation already received, which may be deposited in a checking or savings account, is not subject to the garnishment protections mentioned herein, even if such funds can be traced directly to compensation received.

Generally, the maximum part of the aggregate (from all sources) disposable earnings of an individual for any workweek that is subjected to garnishment may not exceed the lesser of:

1. 25 percent of disposable earnings for that week
2. Amount by which disposable earnings for that week exceed thirty times the federal minimum hourly wage in effect at the time earnings are payable

For example:

1. If your disposable earnings for a workweek totaled $150.00, 25 percent of $150.00 = $37.50; or
2. 30 × $3.80 (based on April 1, 1990, federal minimum hourly wage) = $114.00; $150.00 (disposable earnings) − $114.00 = $36.00
3. Maximum amount subject to garnishment is $36.00, since it is the lesser of $37.50 and $36.00

The above restrictions do not apply to:

- Any order for the support of any person issued by a court of competent jurisdiction or in accordance with an administrative procedure established by state law, which affords substantial due process and is subject to judicial review
- Any order of any court of the United States having jurisdiction under chapter 13 of Title 11 (bankruptcy)
- Any debt due for any state or federal tax

Special rules also apply in cases where earnings are subject to garnishment to enforce any order for the support of another person.

If you are subject to garnishment, you are also protected against discharge from employment because your earnings have been subjected to garnishment for any single indebtedness. Such employment protection is not extended, however, if you have multiple garnishments based on more than one indebtedness. Any employer who willfully fires an employee because of the pendency of a single garnishment can be fined up to $1000, or imprisoned for up to one year, or both.

What is subject to garnishment? Most earnings are subject to garnishment. This includes compensation paid or payable for personal services, such as wages, salaries, commissions, bonuses, and the like. Also included are periodic payments pursuant to pension and retirement plans, including federal pension benefits. Vacation pay also constitutes earnings subject to garnishment. However, unemployment compensation; welfare payments; veterans', disability, and Social Security benefits; and income tax refunds are not considered earnings and are not subject to garnishment.

What are disposable earnings? Disposable earnings are your earnings which remain after the deduction of any amounts required by law to be withheld. Thus, disposable earnings are what you have left from your pay after federal income and Social Security taxes, any state and local taxes are deducted. Amounts *not* "required by law to be withheld" include court-ordered alimony and child support payments and other garnishments.

How does a wage garnishment work? Once a creditor has obtained a final court judgment, a document called a Writ of Attachment of Wages can be executed by the court. This writ is an order notifying your employer of the garnishment. It requires your employer to withhold the applicable portion of your disposable income before any direct payment is made to you. This process will continue until the amount of the garnishment is satisfied in full. On satisfaction, the garnishment ceases.

Check your own state's wage garnishment statute to determine your rights under state law. States have enacted wage garnishment statutes that limit the amount of wages creditors can take toward repayment of an obligation. Where state and federal governments have both enacted provisions limiting garnishment of wages, the statute that protects the *greater* amount of the debtor's earnings from garnishment will be controlling. Thus, federal law provides minimum protections, while the states are free to provide additional protections to their citizens.

In addition, if there are several unsatisfied garnishments against you, state law will prescribe the order in which the garnishments are to be satisfied. Most states give precedence to garnishments according to the order in which they were received.

Execution and Judgment Liens.   Wage garnishment represents one type of judicial lien available to a creditor as a postjudgment execution remedy. The other two types of judicial liens are execution liens and judgment liens. Execution liens relate to a creditor's rights concerning your personal property. Such a lien must be specifically approved, upon motion by your creditor, by the court. Judgment liens relate to real property you own, and they arise automatically with the rendering of a judgment against you. Under these two types of liens, your property will be seized and sold by the sheriff, with the proceeds being distributed to your judgment creditor.

Bankruptcy

Under federal bankruptcy law, you may be allowed to avoid or alter your obligations to creditors and their potential remedies against you. Bankruptcy protection is intended to give you a "fresh start" so you can resume your life out from under the cloud of overwhelming indebtedness.

Many people, when confronted with a sizable debt problem, look toward bankruptcy as a preferred way of dispensing with their credit problems. However, bankruptcy is appropriate for only a small percentage of people—those truly in dire financial straits. Bankruptcy protection should be viewed as an extreme or extraordinary solution. It should only be used by people whose debts are so large that there is no realistic prospect of repayment. If there are other options available for managing your debts (like those mentioned in chapter 6), try them first before declaring bankruptcy. Bankruptcy should be viewed as a last resort and should only be turned to after all other attempts to resolve credit problems have failed.

Many people view bankruptcy as an "easy way out." While filing bankruptcy may result in the clearing out of your debts and provide you with a clean slate, it has some very definite disadvantages as well.

First and foremost, is it really prudent for you to be quickly absolved of these obligations? Since you incurred these debts, it is probably in your best interest to repay them. If you use bankruptcy as a "quick fix," will you have learned financial responsibility so you can avoid credit problems in the future? One therapeutic effect of working through your debts and paying them off over time is the respect it teaches for credit. Also, making amends to your creditors through a repayment plan helps to restore your self-esteem. Conversely, bankruptcy carries with it stigmas—guilt, downfall, an embarrassing label or scar—that may only serve further to undermine faltering self-esteem. Bankruptcy, by circumventing the repayment process, allows you to skip these important steps.

Declaring bankruptcy will have a negative impact on your credit report for years to come. Under the federal Fair Credit Reporting Act, all types of bankruptcies will remain on your credit report for ten years from the date of entry of the order for relief or the date of the bankruptcy adjudication. This is three years longer than most other types of obligations will be reported. Thus, obtaining future loans will be more difficult, if not impossible.

Declaring bankruptcy will not automatically remove from your credit report the individual obligations dealt with in a bankruptcy proceeding. These may remain on your credit report for the maximum period of time allowed, but no longer than seven years (see chapter 9).

Contrary to what you may think, a bankruptcy may not necessarily dissolve all your debts. Some types of debts— such as alimony, maintenance, child support, educational loans, taxes (including income, property, withholding, and employment taxes), fines, penalties, or forfeitures payable to the government, some punitive damages, and debts based on fraud—are exempt from bankruptcy. Thus, while your other debts *may* be discharged, you will remain liable on these exempt obligations. What's more, since three types of bankruptcy proceedings are available to an individual, you are not necessarily assured that filing bankruptcy will remove all of your debt obligations.

Types of Bankruptcy Proceedings. Under a Chapter 7 filing (liquidation), you are required to surrender most of your property (irrespective of where it is located or who holds it) to a court-appointed trustee. This includes any property you own that is not exempt under federal or state law. Check with your state law to determine if your state follows the federal exemptions or has identified certain limited, exempted property that you are allowed to keep under state law.

Your surrendered property will be liquidated or sold, with the proceeds being distributed to creditors. Each creditor receives an appropriate portion, known as the "bankruptcy dividend," which is equal to the total amount of property in your estate divided by the amount of total claims. In exchange for the above surrender, you are discharged from all your prebankruptcy debts (with the exception of those mentioned above which specifically cannot be absolved through bankruptcy).

Under a Chapter 11 filing (reorganization), you are allowed to attempt a financial reorganization without having to surrender your assets or control of your business. A Chapter 11 filing is designed to give you the opportunity to reorganize (hopefully to generate future profits) instead of letting creditors dismantle your business.

If you have fairly regular income, you may be permitted to attempt a personal reorganization through a Chapter 13 filing (individual debt adjustment). Under such a filing, you will retain control and possession of your assets (rather than having to surrender them to a trustee). You will be required to present a repayment plan to the bankruptcy court under which most or all of your debts will be repaid via payments to a court-appointed trustee. At the end of the payment plan (which typically runs three years), you will be discharged from all your prebankruptcy debts (except exempted obligations and certain long-term commitments). A Chapter 13 filing is used primarily by people trying to save their homes from foreclosure or who have certain nondischargeable debts under a Chapter 7 filing.

By using a Chapter 13 reorganization plan, you are making a conscientious effort to repay debts you incurred. Thus, even though a Chapter 13 bankruptcy will be reflected on your credit report for ten years, you can always point out to future creditors that you did ultimately pay these debts off yourself, rather than having them dissolved altogether under a Chapter 7 filing. This should serve as a demonstration of your commitment to repay obligations you incur.

Which Type of Bankruptcy Is Best for You?   Since a Chapter 11 filing relates primarily to businesses, the two types of bankruptcy proceedings most frequently used by individual debtors are Chapter 7 and 13 filings. When determining which filing should be used, bankruptcy courts assess your ability to repay. If you are able to pay a substantial portion of your debt over the next three years, then you may be required to make a Chapter 13 filing. A bankruptcy court will not allow you to casually dismiss your indebtedness if it thinks you can repay. Thus, if the bankruptcy court decides a Chapter 13 filing is appropriate for you, you could still wind up paying your debts through a wage earner bankruptcy plan. If you are unable to pay a substantial portion of your debts over three years, you may use Chapter 7 or 13 filings or other remedies available under state law.

Bankruptcy can be either voluntary or involuntary. A voluntary bankruptcy case is initiated by a debtor with the filing of a bankruptcy petition. An involuntary bankruptcy petition—forcing a debtor into bankruptcy—can be filed by some of the debtor's creditors. Involuntary bankruptcy can only be accomplished through Chapter 7 or 11 filings. You cannot be forced into involuntary bankruptcy under Chapter 13.

How a Bankruptcy Works. Once a bankruptcy petition is filed, creditors are automatically "stayed" or temporarily postponed from proceeding against you. Although certain exceptions exist, this generally means that creditors cannot, on prepetition claims:

- Begin or continue legal or administrative proceedings against you
- Enforce any prepetition judgments against you or your property
- Create, perfect, or enforce a lien against your property
- Take possession or exercise control over your property or
- Collect any claims against you that arose before the petition

The above stay will remain in effect until the property ceases to be property of the estate or the bankruptcy case has been closed, dismissed, or the debtor receives a discharge. While creditors are prohibited from proceeding against you on the above *pre*petition claims, nothing precludes a creditor from proceeding against you on obligations which arose *after* the filing of the bankruptcy petition.

When the bankruptcy trial or proceeding is completed, the balance of each debt you owe to your creditors is generally discharged. Such a discharge operates to void any judgment obtained against you that was the subject of the bankruptcy petition, and operates as an injunction against the commencement or continuation of any action to recover prebankruptcy debts. Then your "fresh start" begins.

Consult an Attorney. Bankruptcy involves very complicated legal issues. It is also one of life's major decisions. Thus, you must base your decision about whether to declare bankruptcy on competent legal advice. Should you wish to pursue bankruptcy, consult an attorney who specializes in bankruptcy before proceeding. Make sure you know exactly what you're getting into before you take actions you may regret later.

CHAPTER 8

Borrowing Money to Pay Outstanding Credit Obligations

This chapter discusses borrowing money through various financing mechanisms to pay outstanding credit obligations. Whether you pay your bills with the proceeds of a home equity or bill consolidation loan, with money provided by others, or through savings, you should *never* view your funding source as extra income. The money is not income; you are simply borrowing to pay bills you have already incurred.

If you use such funding, *you should not undertake any new credit liability until your funding source is repaid in full.* If you continue to use credit, you are simply digging yourself a deeper hole and will probably end up in a far worse situation than you were in before you obtained the funding.

Therefore, before borrowing money to pay your bills, you must:

- Be absolutely certain you have the self-discipline to forgo new credit entirely until the funding source is paid in full

- Make a commitment to yourself and others (spouse, partner, relative, friend, banker) to repay the funding source before assuming any new debts; to demonstrate this commitment, you might consider signing a non-binding "contract," similar to the one below:

Commitment to Repay

I, _____, have borrowed money from
(debtor's name)

_____, to pay
(lender's name)

outstanding bills. I hereby promise to repay every penny of this money I have borrowed before I incur *any* new debts.

_____   _____
(debtor's signature)   (date)

If you do not have the discipline, are unwilling to make the commitment, or have any doubt that you will be able to refrain from further indebtedness, don't borrow money to pay your bills. You will be better off in the long run.

Home Equity Loans

As the result of 1986 tax reform, home equity loans have become perhaps the hottest credit products available. This is because home equity loans are one of the last remaining tax loopholes available to consumers. Under current tax rules, if you have amassed equity in your home, you can take out a home equity loan and may be able to deduct all the interest you pay on this loan. And, since the consumer interest deduction is being winnowed down and will be totally eliminated by 1991, some consumers are reorganizing their debts away from nondeductible obligations and toward deductible home equity loan interest expenses.

Given this fact, many financial institutions are currently vigorously advertising for home equity loan business. Creative, new home equity loan products, with varying features, are emerging daily. Variable-interest home equity loans abound; others come with fixed interest rates; some offer low monthly payments with balloon payments at the end of the loan. With some home equity loans, you can even write checks or use a credit card that accesses the equity you have in your home. Preapproved lines of credit attached to your home's equity hold forth the promise of never having to apply for another loan.

Since offerings vary tremendously, you must carefully evaluate home equity loan products before taking out such loans. Shop around to find the loan that best suits your individual needs. Consider the following information when you scrutinize various home equity loan products.

Evaluate Your Options

Have you explored the possibility of borrowing money from other sources so you can avoid the use of a home equity loan? Before committing yourself to a home equity loan, consider all the options available to you. If your borrowing needs are fairly meager, maybe you should consider pursuing a personal unsecured loan. Similarly, would a second mortgage, with fixed interest rates and payment amounts, be more appropriate? Does borrowing money from others and using your accumulated savings make more sense than mortgaging your home?

Check with a Tax Adviser Before Obtaining a Home Equity Loan

Since the deductibility of interest is perhaps the most compelling reason for getting a home equity loan, you should consult a tax adviser *before* applying for such a loan. Generally, you should be able to deduct your interest expenses on a home equity loan. However, the tax rules concerning deductibility do not lend themselves to simple explanation.

For example, interest expenses on home equity loans are fully deductible only on amounts borrowed against the original purchase price of your home up to $100,000. If your home's value has increased, your lender has based your loan on your home's current market value, and your home equity loan is in excess of the amount you originally paid for your house, then all your interest expenses will *not* be deductible. The following example illustrates this point:

Original purchase price of your home	$50,000
Current market value of your home	$100,000
Amount of home equity loan	$75,000

In the example above, you will be able fully to deduct interest paid on the first $50,000 of your loan; interest you paid on the remaining $25,000 will *not* be fully deductible but subject to the rules governing the deductibility of consumer interest.

Consider a Home Equity Loan Only *if You Are Financially Responsible*

Do *not* take out a home equity loan, or even consider one, if you are in any way irresponsible with money. If you obtain a home equity loan to pay bills, *do not incur any new debt until the home equity loan is paid off*! The risks are simply too great to play around with the equity in your home. If you take out a home equity loan and continue to run up other debts, you are compounding your credit problems and risking the loss of your home. So if you are not financially responsible, it is far better to stop the madness before you end up on the street.

Be Knowledgeable About Interest Rates

Many of the current home equity products are variable-interest offerings (the interest rate fluctuates with economic conditions), which appear to carry phenomenally low interest rates. While some advertisements tout rates as low as 3.9 percent, numerous others are offered in the 5.9 percent to 6.9 percent range. Most of these rates, however, are simply promotional rates, available through a certain date or for a set period of time—normally ninety days. After the promotional period, the actual rate will usually be indexed to an outside rate, like the prime lending rate, with a specified percentage added. Thus, you may only benefit from the promotional rate for a short period of time, with the bulk of your loan coming at a substantially higher interest rate.

This actual rate may still be lower than anything else you can obtain on the market. And, since your indebtedness is linked to an outside index, you might benefit from an even lower rate in the future. Conversely, if interest rates rise, you might end up paying a higher interest rate on this obligation.

Be Wary of Long-Term Loans at Variable Interest Rates

If you take out a variable-rate home equity loan, you should be wary of the uncertainties of changing economic conditions. Do not take out a long-term home equity loan just on the off chance that interest rates will remain low. Should you obtain an open-end home equity loan, don't use more of your approved line of credit than you can realistically repay in a couple of years. Or, if you get a closed-end loan (fixed payments over a certain period), take out a short-term loan—two to three years. Then, if interest rates skyrocket, you should be able to pay off your obligation fairly quickly. If you need to borrow more money, you will be able to base your decision on the economic conditions of the time rather than being locked into a high interest rate under a long-term loan.

Be Aware of Hidden Costs

Since home equity loans relate to an interest in real estate, they carry the same sorts of expenses you would normally encounter when buying a house—such as closing costs, appraisal fees, title searches, points (a percentage of the amount borrowed), attorneys' fees, and so on. You should also be on the lookout for other costs your lender may attach to the loan, for example, application fees, annual fees, transaction charges, and service charges. In addition, be aware that some home equity loans carry prepayment penalties. You will need to consider such costs when deciding whether to apply for a home equity loan.

Other Considerations

Many home equity loans require relatively high minimum loan amounts, normally $5,000 or more. Thus, it may be impractical to use a home equity loan if you need to borrow a relatively small amount. Some loans also carry maximum or minimum withdrawal requirements. In addition, lenders place an outside limit on the percentage of equity in your home you can access. Most lenders will only allow you to borrow around 75 to 80 percent of your home's current market value, minus any encumbrances (like your first mortgage and any second mortgages). Also, some lenders' income requirements for home equity loans tend to be higher than those required for an unsecured loan. For example, a lender might require the homeowner to have sufficient income to pay off the outstanding line of credit. If your loan has a variable interest rate, you should check to see whether you are allowed to convert it from a variable rate to a fixed rate.

Your Right to Timely Disclosure of Home Equity Loan Pricing Information

Creditors are required to disclose most of the above information to you *before* you enter into any home equity loan agreement. This is to assure you have access to crucial information in a timely fashion so you can make prudent decisions. Creditors are also prohibited from engaging in certain unfair practices, like unilaterally changing the contractual terms of your agreement after it has been signed. In addition, if home equity lenders advertise key pricing components of their offerings, they must also disclose other relevant pricing information in the same advertisement.

Bill Consolidation Loans

A bill consolidation loan may be an alternative available to some people experiencing credit difficulty. Through such a loan, a lender can provide you with money to pay some or all of your bills. Bill payments may be simplified with a single monthly payment to one creditor. These payments, which are normally stretched out over a two- to three-year period, may be lower than the bills you were paying individually each month. This could give you a little more flexibility in meeting monthly obligations and in responding to emergencies. It could also save you the trouble of developing repayment plans with individual creditors.

If you are interested in a bill consolidation loan, check with several financial institutions to see what types of loans they offer, and select the one most appropriate for you.

Types of Bill Consolidation Loans

There are two types of bill consolidation loans. The true bill consolidation loan is used for the express purpose of paying outstanding bills. The financial institution writes a new loan for the amount of the indebtedness, closes outstanding accounts, and makes payments directly to creditors on your behalf. The other, more prevalent type of bill consolidation loan is a personal unsecured loan, under which the financial institution pays loan proceeds directly to you. Since you control the ultimate destination of the loan money, funds may be used to pay creditors, purchase a new appliance, make car repairs, or for other purposes.

Since some financial institutions are reluctant to write loans if the sole purpose is bill consolidation, your best bet is to apply for a personal unsecured loan and use the proceeds for bill consolidation purposes.

Loan Length Limits

Since most bill consolidation loans are unsecured, lenders will normally not extend credit beyond 15 percent of your annual take-home pay. In addition, these loans are rarely available for long periods of time, with maximum loan lengths of two to three years being common.

Eligibility

For many people experiencing credit difficulty, a bill consolidation loan is not a realistic alternative. If you have a bad credit rating, lenders may refuse to extend you credit. Even if your credit rating is still good, your outstanding indebtedness may make you overextended. As the result, you may be unable to obtain credit on reasonable terms.

Reasonable Terms

A bill consolidation loan should only be undertaken if you can *reduce* the rates of interest paid on all bills you wish to consolidate. Before considering a bill consolidation loan, enter all outstanding obligations with relevant information on the chart below.

Name of Creditor/Type of Loan	Current Balance	Rate of Interest
_____	$_____	____%
_____	$_____	____%
_____	$_____	____%
_____	$_____	____%
_____	$_____	____%
_____	$_____	____%
_____	$_____	____%
_____	$_____	____%
_____	$_____	____%
_____	$_____	____%

Let's assume you qualify for an unsecured, personal loan at a 12 percent rate of interest, and your total indebtedness is as follows:

Name of Creditor/Type of Loan	Current Balance	Rate of Interest
Store charge	$1,500	21.0%
Credit card #1	$2,000	19.8%
Credit card #2	$ 500	18.9%
Personal loan	$1,000	16.0%
Student loan	$4,000	7.0%
Car loan	$8,000	2.9%

Since the car and student loans carry interest rates that are less than the rate of interest on the consolidation loan, neither of these should be consolidated. The remaining 4 loans can be consolidated into a $5,000 loan. This will reduce the rates of interest you are paying by a minimum of 4.5 to a maximum of 9.5 percentage points, which will save you money. In addition, this loan should yield monthly payments of approximately $235.40 for a 24-month loan or $166.10 for a 36-month loan.

However, since the total indebtedness above is $17,000, you're probably overextended. In fact, your gross income would have to be in excess of $200,000 a year for this indebtedness to fall within tolerable limits.

As a result, it may be difficult if not impossible to find a financial institution that will make you a loan. Since financial institutions—banks, savings and loans, or credit unions—normally offer the best interest rates on unsecured loans, you may be unable to obtain a loan on favorable terms.

You might try to obtain a loan through a finance company, if you can find one that offers a favorable interest rate. However, while most loans from financial institutions hover a few points above the prime lending rate, some finance companies charge 21 percent and upwards for unsecured loans. This is because finance companies often cater to high risk individuals who cannot get credit elsewhere. In addition, finance company loans may appear enticing because of their lower monthly payments, due to longer repayment periods. But longer repayment periods result in higher ultimate interest costs to you.

Therefore, if the only loan you can get is from a finance company with a high interest rate, do not take out a new loan. You will be better off negotiating a repayment plan directly with your creditors, following the steps outlined in chapter 6.

Paying Bills with Money Provided by Others

A relative or close friend may prove to be a convenient loan source. Such a credit extension can be very helpful in seeing you through a crisis, particularly since you may be able to obtain more favorable terms than you could get from a financial institution. In fact, these loans are often extended with no expectation of interest or with an interest rate that approximates what your benefactor would have earned on the money through savings. Even if the interest rate is comparable to those being charged by financial institutions, the loan may still be in your best interest since you may be unable to get credit on similar terms from another source.

However, if you qualify for a loan on favorable terms at a financial institution, you should probably choose that option. Timely repayment of such a loan will likely be reported on your credit report, while the loan from a relative or friend will not. At the same time, you will be establishing a relationship with a financial institution that may be useful in the future.

Financial entanglements can quickly strain family relations or ruin a friendship. If you wish to proceed with this type of loan, it is crucial that the terms of the agreement be set out in writing before any money ever changes hands. *Both parties must be totally aware of all rights and responsibilities.* A basic promissory note should be entered into that will protect the interests of both parties and circumvent any potential misunderstandings about the terms of the agreement.

Sample Promissory Note

Date: _____

City: _____

State: _____

I, _____ , _____
    (full name of debtor)   (address)

_____

(city, state, zip code)

(__) _____ , _____ , _____ ,
(telephone number)   (Social Security number)   (date of birth)

do hereby acknowledge the receipt of a cash loan from

_____ , in the amount of

(full name of creditor)

_____ dollars ($ _____), made on

(amount of loan)

_____ . The purpose of this loan is: _____

(date of loan)

_____ .

I promise to pay to the order of _____

(full name of creditor)

_____ ,

(address, city, state, zip code)

(__) _____ , the sum of _____ dollars,

(telephone number)   (amount of loan)

($ _____), in _____ (__) equal installments of

(number of installments)

_____ dollars ($_____) each, with a final payment of
(amount of payment)

_____ dollars ($_____), due on _____
(amount of final payment)   (date)

Interest shall be payable at the rate of _____ percent (%)

simple interest. Payment shall be due on the _____ ( )

day of each month beginning on _____.
                                          (date payments begin)

Any payment not received by the _____ ( ) day

of the month in which it is due shall be considered in default. As a result of the default of *any* payment due under this note, _____, or any holder of this
                            (name of creditor)

note, may declare the entire note due and demand immediate payment in full of the outstanding balance of the note. Further interest shall accrue at the rate of _____ percent (%)

simple interest on the unpaid balance from the date of such demand until payment in full. Any holder of this note shall also be entitled to collection costs, court costs, and reasonable attorneys' fees.

_____
(full signature of debtor)

_____
(date signed)

Paying Bills with Savings

A simple solution for some people confronted with a debt crisis is to pay all or some debts with accumulated savings. If you have savings, this may be an appropriate option. For many savers, however, there may be compelling reasons not to use savings for the payment of debts. Obviously, if you have no savings, this alternative is not available to you.

Before dipping into your savings, determine if the use of

these funds is actually in your best interest. Make certain that the use of savings is not simply "the easy way out" or a convenient way of dealing with the problem. The existence of savings indicates you can be responsible in handling money. Most creditors will look more favorably upon a credit application if prudent savings practices are apparent. Therefore, if you can see yourself clear of the problem without having to resort to savings, you should.

Savings is also an excellent way of planning ahead. The use of savings to pay bills might leave you and your family with limited recourse should an emergency arise. If you choose to use savings, either set a small portion of it aside or start a new, modest savings program so you will be prepared for the unexpected. Should you decide to dip into your savings to pay bills, don't let this discourage future saving. Resume prudent savings practices as soon as your current debt crisis has been resolved. View the use of savings to pay bills as a loan to yourself, and devise a definite repayment plan, just as you would with an ordinary loan.

Using savings may be appropriate if you are paying high rates of interest on credit obligations and earning low rates of interest on savings instruments. For example, if your credit card interest rates are in the 16 to 24 percent range, and you have a passbook savings account earning 5.25 percent interest, you might seriously consider using some portion of your accumulated savings to pay outstanding credit obligations. If the rate you are *earning on your savings account* is far less than the rate you are *paying on your credit obligations*, you may be losing ground in your fight for solvency.

If, on the other hand, you have a certificate of deposit earning 17 percent interest (which cannot be renewed at that rate), do not use this particular savings instrument to pay debts. You should hold onto it and figure out some other way to pay your bills.

Familiarize yourself with your financial institution's policies concerning penalties, service charges, or fees that may be imposed due to withdrawal from savings. For example, if a substantial penalty will be imposed for early withdrawal, you are probably better off not using the savings source. Similarly, if you are required to maintain a minimum balance in your bank account to avoid additional fees or earn a higher interest rate, make certain to maintain this balance.

Prepayment Penalties

A prepayment penalty is assessed on some loans if you pay the loan off early. The purpose of such a penalty is to assure the creditor an adequate rate of return on their extension of credit to you. By paying a loan off early, you are saving the amount of money you would have paid in interest during the remainder of the loan. This means your creditor will make less profit on the loan because of your prepayment. Prepayment penalties cannot be assessed unless they are specifically called for in the credit agreement or note evidencing the debt.

Before paying any loans prior to their maturation date, make sure a prepayment penalty will not be assessed. If one will be, evaluate whether the money you will save through prepayment is more than the penalty you will pay. You should also be aware that prepayment penalties are not tax-deductible.

CHAPTER 9

Your Credit Report

Have you ever had a loan application denied? If so, you probably felt humiliated that some omnipotent creditor had decided you were a bad credit risk—that you were unworthy of an extension of credit.

When evaluating your application, your creditor will probably have relied on information contained in a credit report from a credit-reporting agency (also known as a credit bureau). If the decision was based on such a report, the creditor must advise you of this fact. The boldfaced portion of the sample rejection letter below illustrates this point:

Dear_____:

We regret to inform you that your recent request for an XYZ charge account has been declined for the following reasons:

_____ Credit application incomplete
_____ Insufficient number of credit references provided
_____ Unacceptable type of credit references provided
_____ Unable to verify credit references
_____ Temporary or irregular employment
_____ Unable to verify employment
_____ Length of employment
_____ Income insufficient for amount of credit requested
_____ Excessive obligations in relation to income

_____ Unable to verify income
_____ Length of residence
_____ Temporary residence
_____ Unable to verify residence
_____ No credit file
_____ Limited credit experience
_____ Poor credit performance with us
_____ Delinquent past or present credit obligations with others
_____ Garnishment, attachment, foreclosure, repossession, collection action, or judgment
_____ Bankruptcy
_____ Value or type of collateral not sufficient
_____ Other: _____

In determining your creditworthiness, we relied, in whole or in part, on information provided to us by the following credit-reporting agency:

_____

_____

_____

Under the Fair Credit Reporting Act, you have the right to know the information contained in your credit file. Any questions regarding such information should be directed to the credit-reporting agency above.

NOTICE: The federal Equal Credit Opportunity Act prohibits creditors from discriminating against credit applicants on the basis of race, color, religion, national origin, sex, marital status, age (provided the applicant has the capacity to enter into a binding contract); because all or part of the applicant's income derives from any public assistance program; or because the applicant has in good faith exercised any right under the Consumer Protection Act. The federal agency that administers compliance with this law concerning this creditor is:

_____.

The Importance of a Sound Credit History

Since access to credit has become indispensable in today's society, your creditworthiness is an important part of your identity. A sound credit history, which allows you access to credit, is essential to providing you with a strong financial base from which to attain your goals.

If you have blemishes on your credit report, you may be unable to buy a home, purchase a car, obtain a credit card, or borrow money for your child's education. You may feel like a convicted felon—a marked person who is plagued by a tainted past. You might fear that your credit report will prevent you from ever receiving credit again.

The Importance of Reviewing Your Credit History

While people who are having or have had repayment problems certainly need to become familiar with their credit histories, it is also important for those people who have never had any problems repaying obligations in a timely fashion to review their credit files periodically. A review of your credit history might well reveal inaccurate or incomplete information. If this is the case, with a few simple steps, you may be able to clear up your credit rating and restore your creditworthiness.

For example, you may have paid off one of your creditors, but your credit report still reflects a substantial balance due. As a result, prospective creditors may view you as overextended. By revising the balance-due figure to reflect your current zero balance, you are strengthening your credit report. Similarly, you might be able to minimize the damage of any unfavorable information that is being reported through the inclusion of a personal statement explaining the reasons. Everyone should routinely review his or her own credit file at least once every two to three years.

What Are Credit-Reporting Agencies?

Credit-reporting agencies (also commonly referred to as credit bureaus) gather, store, and disseminate information relating to the identity, paying habits, and financial well-being of individuals. This information is obtained from creditors who routinely report such information to credit-reporting agencies and from public information available through court records and other public documents.

The role of credit-reporting agencies is to provide creditors with information concerning your creditworthiness. They serve merely as a source or library of information concerning your financial well-being. Credit-reporting agencies provide information concerning your past performance, which can then be used as a predictor of future performance by potential creditors. They do not decide whether your credit application should be accepted or denied. Rather, based on information provided by credit-reporting agencies, prospective creditors, applying their own credit-granting criteria, determine the fate of your credit application.

Since credit-reporting agencies maintain credit files on millions of people, they are highly automated facilities, with most activities occurring through computerized transmittals.

Which Credit-Reporting Agencies Maintain Files on You?

More than one credit-reporting agency may be maintaining a file on you. Since credit-reporting agencies maintain separate, independent files, clearing up a problem with one credit-reporting agency has *no* effect on how this same information may be reported by another.

Ask a local banker or merchant for the names and addresses of the credit-reporting agencies that serve your local area. You can also check with your local Chamber of Commerce, Better Business Bureau, or Retail Merchants Association (if one exists in your local area). Or contact the four largest credit-reporting agencies, at the addresses below, to determine if they maintain a file on you:

TRW Credit Data
505 City Parkway West, Suite 110
Orange, CA 92613–5450
(714)991–6000

The Credit Bureau, Inc.
(also known as CBI/Equifax)
5501 Peachtree Dunwoody Road, Suite 600
Atlanta, GA 30356
(404)250–4000

Trans Union Credit Information Company
444 North Michigan Avenue
Chicago, IL 60611
(312)645–0012

CSC Credit Services, Inc.
652 East North Belt, Suite 133
Houston, TX 77060
(713)878–4840

The above are the headquarters of these companies. Your request will probably be referred to the regional office that maintains files for your local area. Since the above telephone numbers access busy, computerized switchboards, it is probably best to make your request in writing, saving yourself long-distance telephone charges.

A look at your local yellow pages (in a rural area, the yellow pages of the largest city near you) under "Credit-Reporting Agencies" will also probably reveal the names of several credit-reporting agencies that serve your area. Some of these will be smaller firms that maintain local or regional files; others may be the major agencies. Be aware that some of the firms listed in the yellow pages may be limited in scope (for example, they may only provide mortgage-related credit information). Thus, if you use the yellow pages, be on the lookout for the names of the major credit-reporting agencies above, or ask, when you call, if the agencies compile comprehensive consumer credit information. Once you have found a credit-reporting agency that maintains a file on you, you might also ask them for the names of other credit-reporting agencies that are likely to have your credit history on file.

If the above actions fail to reveal a credit-reporting agency that maintains files on you, you can always request this information from:

Associated Credit Bureaus, Inc.
Member Services Department
PO Box 218300
Houston, TX 77218
(713)492–8155

What Information Is Contained in Your Credit Report?

Credit reports contain information about the types of credit accounts you may have; your past and present repayment activities on loans, charge accounts, credit cards, and other extensions of credit; and whether you have ever filed bank-ruptcy or been sued. However, since some creditors do not report, or may only report certain accounts (that is, delin-quent accounts), to credit-reporting agencies, some of your accounts may *not* appear on your credit report.

Accounts with the following types of credit providers will *normally appear* on your credit report: major credit cards, major financial institutions (like banks, savings and loans, credit unions), major department stores, finance and loan companies, and collection agencies. The following types of obligations *normally do not appear* on your credit report: small financial institutions, home mortgages, utility companies (telephone, electric, gas), oil/gas companies, rent, medical bills (doctor, dentist, hospital), and other professional bills (lawyer, accountant, and so on). While the preceding obliga-tions may not routinely be reported to a credit-reporting agency, their likelihood of being reported increases precipi-tously should you default on such obligations. (The above are obviously general categories and will vary depending on your creditors' reporting practices.)

Public record information that may be reflected on your credit report includes bankruptcies, garnishments, tax liens, and court judgments. Information on banking activities, like checking or savings accounts, will not appear on your credit report.

How Long Does Information Appear on Your Credit Report?

Favorable Information

Credit-reporting agencies are under no time restrictions for reporting favorable credit information. Thus, if you had a car loan ten years ago that you paid according to the terms of your agreement, favorable information concerning this loan might still appear on your credit report.

In addition, any current accounts you may have will remain on your credit report indefinitely. These include your revolving charge cards, credit cards, open-end loans, or lines of credit.

Adverse Information

Credit-reporting agencies are prohibited from reporting adverse information beyond certain, prescribed time periods. The following types of information can only be reported for the indicated periods:

Delinquent accounts—seven years. A delinquent account (that has neither been placed for collection nor charged to profit and loss) may be reported for seven years from the date of the last regularly scheduled payment.

Accounts placed for collection—seven years. The seven-year period begins when the creditor initiates internal collection activity or refers the account to an outside collector, whichever occurs first.

Accounts charged to profit and loss—seven years. For such accounts, the seven-year clock begins to run from the date the creditor takes action to write off the account.

Lawsuits—seven years. Lawsuits shall not be reported for more than seven years from the date the suit was initiated, unless the governing statute of limitations has not expired.

Judgments—seven years. Judgments may only be reported for seven years from the date the judgment was rendered.

Bankruptcies—ten years. All types of bankruptcy will remain on your credit report for ten years from the date of entry of the order for relief or the date of adjudication.

Your Right to Review Your Credit Report

Everyone has the right to review his or her own credit report. Upon request and proper identification, every credit-reporting agency must clearly and accurately disclose to the consumer:

- The nature and substance of all information in its files on the consumer at the time of the request
- The sources of the information
- The recipients of any credit-related consumer reports it has furnished during the last six months

Costs of Credit Reports

If you have been declined credit within the last thirty days, the credit-reporting agency that provided your prospective creditor a copy of your credit report must disclose to you *without charge* the contents of this report. The identity of the credit-reporting agency that furnished this information should be clearly indicated on the rejection letter from your creditor.

If you have *not* been declined credit within the last thirty days, you may still review the contents of your credit file, provided you pay a fee. Costs range from five to twenty dollars, depending on the credit-reporting agency and the state in which you live.

Reviewing Your Credit Report

To enable you to evaluate the contents of your credit file thoroughly, make every effort to obtain a written copy of your credit report. Most major credit-reporting agencies currently provide written copies of credit reports to consumers. In addition, some state laws require the written disclosure of credit file information. However, federal law does *not* require these consumer disclosures to be made in writing.

You may review the contents of your credit report via one of the following three methods:

• **In person.** A person may review his or her credit file at the consumer reporting agency during normal business hours and on reasonable notice, provided proper identification is furnished. Make an appointment, and bring the required identification

• **By telephone.** Before telephone disclosure can occur, you must first make a written request, with proper identification. In addition, you are responsible for any telephone charges that may be incurred. Often recorded messages, busy signals, and long hold periods make this the least desirable way of dealing with a credit-reporting agency

• **By mail.** If you have been declined credit within the past thirty days, send a copy of your creditor's rejection letter to the appropriate credit-reporting agency. Indicate that you want a copy of your credit report. Make sure that you include all pertinent information (like your current mailing address and Social Security number). Also, be sure to sign your request. You might use the following form letter:

Request for Free Copy of Credit Report

Today's date: _____

Your full name: _____

Your current address: _____
(include city/town,
state, zip code) _____

Your former address: _____
(if at your current
address for less than _____
five years)

Your date of birth: _____

Your Social Security number: _____

Dear _____:
       (name of credit-reporting agency)

I was recently declined credit by

_____ on _____
     (name of creditor)   (date of letter)

based upon adverse information contained in a credit file
reported by your agency. Please send me a copy of my credit
report at the above address.
    Thank you.

Sincerely,

(your signature)

Similarly, if you have not been declined credit within the
past thirty days, send a letter to the credit-reporting agency.
Make certain to provide the information included on the
following form:

Request for Copy of Credit Report

Today's date: _____

Your full name: _____

Your current address: _____
(include city/town,
state, zip code) _____

Your former address: _____
(if at your current
address for less than _____
five years)

Your date of birth: _____

Your Social Security number: _____

Dear _____:
        (name of credit-reporting agency)

Please send me a current copy of my credit report
at the above address. I am enclosing a (check/money order)
in the amount of $ _____ to cover the required fee.
                    (amount of fee)
   Thank you.

Sincerely,

(your signature)

Understanding Your Credit Report

Once your credit report has been disclosed to you, if you are
unfamiliar with computer and/or with deciphering credit
reports, you may have your work cut out for you. As the
sample below demonstrates, credit reports can be difficult to
understand.

Often provided on computer paper, credit reports are
usually cluttered with symbols and abbreviations that are
meaningless to the uninitiated reader. Your best bet is to
wade through the explanatory information that accompanies
your credit report. Get a magnifying glass if you must, but it
is well worth your while to understand, and gain a basic
familiarity with, the contents of your credit report.

Credit-reporting agencies are required to provide trained
personnel to explain any information contained in your

NAME AND ADDRESS OF CREDIT BUREAU MAKING REPORT

☐ SINGLE REFERENCE ☒ IN FILE REPORT ☐ TRADE REPORT

☐ FULL REPORT ☐ EMPLOY & TRADE REPORT ☐ PREVIOUS RESIDENCE REPORT

☐ OTHER _____

CREDIT BUREAU OF ANYTOWN
1131 MAIN ST.
ANYTOWN, ANYSTATE 12345

FOR	FIRST NATIONAL BANK ANYTOWN, ANYSTATE 12345

Date Received **4/11/86**
Date Mailed **4/11/86**
In File Since **APRIL 1970**
Inquired As: **JOINT ACCOUNT**

CONFIDENTIAL
crediscope® REPORT

Ⓜ Member
Associated Credit Bureaus, Inc.

REPORT ON: LAST NAME	FIRST NAME	INITIAL	SOCIAL SECURITY NUMBER	SPOUSE'S NAME
CONSUMER	ROBERT	G.	123-45-6789	BETTY R.

ADDRESS: CITY	STATE:	ZIP CODE	SINCE:	SPOUSE'S SOCIAL SECURITY NO.
1234 ANY ST. ANYTOWN	ANYSTATE	12333	1973	987-65-4321

COMPLETE TO HERE FOR TRADE REPORT AND SKIP TO CREDIT HISTORY

PRESENT EMPLOYER:	POSITION HELD:	SINCE:	DATE EMPLOY VERIFIED	EST. MONTHLY INCOME
XYZ CORPORATION	ASST. DEPT. MGR.	10/81	12/81	$2500

COMPLETE TO HERE FOR EMPLOYMENT AND TRADE REPORT AND SKIP TO CREDIT HISTORY

DATE OF BIRTH	NUMBER OF DEPENDENTS INCLUDING SELF:			OTHER: (EXPLAIN)
5/25/50	4	☒ OWNS OR BUYING HOME	☐ RENTS HOME	☐

FORMER ADDRESS:	CITY:	STATE:	FROM:	TO:
4321 FIRST AVE.	ANYTOWN	ANYSTATE	1970	1973

FORMER EMPLOYER:	POSITION HELD:	FROM:	TO:	EST. MONTHLY INCOME
ABC & ASSOCIATES	SALES PERSON	2/80	9/81	$1285

SPOUSE'S EMPLOYER:	POSITION HELD:	SINCE:	DATE EMPLOY VERIFIED	EST. MONTHLY INCOME
BIG CITY DEPT. STORE	CASHIER	4/81	12/81	$1200

CREDIT HISTORY *(Complete this section for all reports)*

WHOSE	KIND OF BUSINESS AND ID CODE	DATE REPORTED AND METHOD OF REPORTING	DATE OPENED	DATE OF LAST PAYMENT	HIGHEST CREDIT OR LAST CONTRACT	PRESENT STATUS BALANCE OWING	PAST DUE AMOUNT	NO. OF PAYMENTS	NO. MONTHS HISTORY REVIEWED	HISTORICAL STATUS TIMES PAST DUE 30-59 DAYS ONLY	60-89 DAYS ONLY	90 DAYS AND OVER	TYPE & TERMS (MANNER OF PAYMENT)	REMARKS
2	CONSUMER'S BANK B 12-345	2/6/86 AUTOMTD.	12/85	1/86	1200	1100	-0-	-0-	2	-0-	-0-	-0-	INSTALLMENT $100/MO.	
3	BIG CITY DEPT. STORE D 54-321	2/10/86 MANUAL	4/81	1/86	300	100	-0-	-0-	12	-0-	-0-	-0-	REVOLVING $ 25/MO.	
1	SUPER CREDIT CARD N 01-234	12/12/85 AUTOMATD.	7/82	11/85	200	100	100	1	12	1	-0-	-0-	OPEN 30-DAY	

PUBLIC RECORD: SMALL CLAIMS CT. CASE #SC1001 PLAINTIFF: ANYWHERE APPLIANCES
AMOUNT $225 PAID 4/4/82
ADDITIONAL INFORMATION: REF. SMALL CLAIMS CT. CASE #SC1001--5/30/82 SUBJECT SAYS CLAIM PAID
UNDER PROTEST. APPLIANCE DID NOT OPERATE PROPERLY.

credit report. Therefore, if there is something you do not understand, do not hesitate to ask for help.

In addition, you are entitled to bring a person of your choosing to help you decipher your credit file. Try to bring someone who is trustworthy and will respect the confidentiality of the information. If you can find somebody who is knowledgeable about credit reports, that would obviously be helpful. Whomever you choose to bring, make sure he or she comes armed with identification, since it will probably be required by the credit-reporting agency. The credit-reporting agency may also require you to furnish a written statement granting permission to discuss your file in another person's presence.

When reviewing your credit report, take time to evaluate each entry. Jot down all adverse information as well as any information you feel is incorrect or incomplete.

Things to Be on the Lookout for When Reviewing Your Credit History

When carefully reviewing your credit report, make certain all the information is accurate. Correct any incorrect background information—such as current and past employment, address information, and salary figures. In addition, pay particular attention to the following key categories appearing on the report. Make sure that:

• **All the accounts listed on your credit report are in fact your own.** Sometimes, due to name similarities and other factors, it is possible for an account to be incorrectly reported on someone else's credit report

• **All outstanding balances listed on your credit report are accurate.** It could be that a particular account has been paid in full, yet is reflected on your credit report as an amount still outstanding. This might make you appear to be over-extended to any future creditors who review your credit report

• **All past-due amounts are correct.** If all your accounts are current, no past-due amounts should be reflected

• **All dates of last activity (DLA), or status dates, are correct.** This is especially important on accounts that carry a negative rating, since these accounts will remain on your credit report for seven years from DLA. The DLA could be the date of your most recent or final payment, date the account was referred to an outside collection agency, date the account was written off by the creditor, date a judgment was obtained, and so on

• **There are no duplicate submissions—reporting the same account twice.** Sometimes account numbers may be transposed or contain minor variations. As the result the same account may appear on your credit report more than once. When questioning such duplicate submissions, you should indicate which submission you consider to be the more accurate

• **All court or public records indicated are accurate.** If you question the validity of this type of entry, you will have to petition the court of appropriate jurisdiction before the entry can be removed from your credit report

• **All account status reports are accurate.** Since these status designations reflect your payment history for each account, they are the most important information contained in your credit report. These designations serve as the primary basis on which a creditor will either grant or deny you credit

Improving Your Credit Report

The best way to develop a solid credit report is to pay your bills in a timely fashion, according to the terms of your loan or account agreements. However, even though you may have a stellar repayment history, a review of your credit report may reveal obligations that you feel are inaccurate or incomplete. By following the recommendations below, you can have a substantial impact on the way such obligations are reported on your credit report. To maximize your input in the contents of your credit report, you must:

- Preserve your rights under the federal Fair Credit Reporting Act
- Contact your creditors directly

Do not expect to be able to clear up your credit report overnight. Correcting incomplete or inaccurate credit-report information will often take a couple of weeks or months. Just be patient and persistent.

Preserving Your Rights Under the Fair Credit Reporting Act

The federal Fair Credit Reporting Act (FCRA) protects your privacy concerning your credit obligations. It also gives you specific rights designed to assure the maximum possible accuracy of items contained in your credit report. It is a self-help law that allows you to challenge the accuracy or completeness of credit-report entries.

The act provides a mechanism for correcting *erroneous* information in your credit file. It does *not* allow you to have an accurately reported negative credit history erased.

To assure the accuracy or completeness of items contained in your credit report, take a critical look at all items reflected in it. Assert your rights about any items with which you disagree or that you believe should be more fully explained.

Disputing Credit Report Information. If you dispute the accuracy or completeness of information contained in your credit report, indicate all such items either on the dispute form or in the spaces provided on the credit report itself. Try to keep these disputes as brief and concise as possible.

You must challenge the accuracy or completeness of items that are currently reflected on your credit report. You cannot argue incompleteness just because an obligation does not appear on your credit report. Rather, you must take issue with the way particular items that currently appear on your credit report *are* reported.

In addition, your dispute must actually challenge the accuracy or completeness of the item of information in your credit file relating to the debt. You cannot merely provide a reason for payment problems—such as the death of a spouse, an illness, the loss of a job, and so on. Rather, your dispute must specifically relate to the information actually being reported. For example, if another person's account is reflected on your credit report, your dispute must go to the accuracy of this entry.

After you have written down all of your disputes, submit them to the credit-reporting agency. Keep a copy for your files, making sure to note the date on which they were mailed.

Credit-Reporting Agencies Must Reinvestigate Disputed Information. By disputing information in your file, you shift the burden for continued inclusion of the information to the credit-reporting agency and the original creditor. Credit-reporting agencies are required to follow reasonable procedures to assure the maximum possible accuracy of information in their files. The credit-reporting agency must reinvestigate and record the current status of disputed information within a reasonable period of time (thirty days) after receiving your dispute.

To conduct its reinvestigation, the credit-reporting agency will contact the original creditor, advise him or her of your dispute, and state your position. The original creditor will then be asked to confirm the information, qualify it, or accept your explanation.

If the original creditor fails to respond to the credit-reporting agency within a reasonable period of time, the disputed information will be deleted from your file, since it can no longer be verified. Similarly, if the creditor accepts your explanation, the disputed information will either be deleted or revised to reflect a more accurate status. However, if the original creditor confirms or qualifies the information, such information or revised information will continue to appear on your credit report.

Your Right to a Statement. If the reinvestigation does not resolve your dispute, you may file a brief statement, for inclusion in your credit file, describing the nature of your dispute. Then, in any subsequent reports containing the adverse information, the credit-reporting agency must clearly note that the information is disputed and provide either your statement or a clear and accurate summary thereof.

If you file a statement, it must relate to the obligation in question and not merely explain extenuating circumstances or present a rationalization for payment problems. In addition, the credit-reporting agency may limit your statement to 100 words (for each disputed item) if it provides you with assistance in writing a clear summary of the dispute.

Your statement should be positive and upbeat. Rather than slamming the creditor with disparaging comments, accentuate your positive actions, like taking responsibility for resolving a difficult matter. The following example demonstrates this point:

This obligation was paid off under a repayment plan voluntarily entered into and mutually agreeable to both parties. Final payment was made on _____, three months earlier than required under the payment plan. The creditor has since reinstated the account, which is now current.

Preparing a statement for inclusion in your credit file affords you the opportunity to tell your side of the story. Thus, creditors will be able to consider your statement alongside the adverse entry.

Your Right to Have Revised Information Communicated to Creditors Who Have Received Your Credit Report During the Last Six Months.   Whether your dispute results in the deletion, revision, or inclusion of a statement explaining adverse information, you have the right to have the credit-reporting agency disclose this new information to creditors who received a copy of your credit report during the last six months. You must request the credit-reporting agency to furnish such revised reports to specifically designated creditors.

Contacting Your Creditors Directly

The above describes how you can dispute items contained in your credit report using the framework specifically provided under the Fair Credit Reporting Act. However, you should also contact all creditors with whom you have a dispute to see if the matter can be resolved directly. Make certain all such communications with creditors are in writing.

Directly contacting your creditors demonstrates your sincerity in wanting to get the matter resolved and personalizes your creditors' frame of reference for you. In addition, since many creditors are computerized, some items must be removed at the source so they will not continue to be reported with the creditor's regular transmittals to credit-reporting agencies.

When contacting your creditors, advise them you have become aware of adverse information they are currently reporting on your credit report. Tell them you feel this information is either inaccurate or incomplete. Explain your version of account activities, providing enough information so that creditors have some logical basis for giving you the benefit of the doubt and granting your request. Suggest solutions you feel would more accurately reflect the status of your account.

You should also tell your creditors that you view the way they report your account as a very serious matter. If you are a current account holder, are a customer of long standing, have other account relationships with the same institution, or are contemplating future activities with the same creditor, let them know that their resolution of your account reporting problem will influence your future activities with their firm. If the creditor does not take your dispute seriously, you may be forced to reevaluate your relationship—by refusing to shop in the creditor's stores or moving your account to a competitor institution.

In addition, since researching and possibly altering your account status will take some effort on your creditors' part, be sure to let them know how much you appreciate their endeavors.

Inquiries

At the end of your credit report, notice the inquiries section. This is simply a listing of creditors who have requested a copy of your credit report. If you request a copy of your credit report, this will also be noted in the inquiry section.

The inquiry section does not indicate whether the creditors who made the inquiries granted or denied you credit. However, you should be aware that some creditors review the inquiries section to see if a large number of inquiries have been made recently. If so, a potential creditor might fear you are attempting to "pad" your credit usage (get more credit than you can realistically repay) and decline your application.

To avoid having potential creditors view a large number of inquiries suspiciously, limit the number of credit applications you submit. If you are applying for an important loan such as a mortgage, you might not want to apply for credit for the six-month to one-year period immediately preceding your mortgage application. This should assure a low number of inquiries (or none) reflected on your credit report.

Credit-reporting agencies are required to maintain a listing of inquiries on your account for at least six months. However, in practice, most retain inquiry listings for two years. After two years, inquiry listings should automatically drop off your credit report.

Delinquency Indicators

A new trend in the credit-reporting industry is an index designed to predict an individual's likelihood of becoming delinquent on credit obligations. To derive this index, the credit-reporting agency takes many factors contained in your credit report (such as repayment activities, income, length of employment, and length of residence) into consideration. Based on these elements, the credit-reporting agency develops a delinquency predictor index that creditors may use when determining your creditworthiness.

Since you have access to information concerning the various elements used to compute your index, you can take steps to improve these individual components. Thus, you can indirectly influence your delinquency predictor index. However, credit-reporting agencies are not required to disclose to you, explain the relevance of, or allow you to dispute the accuracy of your delinquency predictor index. Not all credit-reporting agencies currently use a delinquency predictor index.

Special Credit-Reporting Agency Services

One credit-reporting agency offers a new service called "credentials." With this service (which costs about thirty-five dollars), you are entitled to unlimited copies of your credit report for a year from the credit-reporting agency, notification whenever anyone makes an inquiry on your credit report, an opportunity to create a consumer financial profile, and a credit card registration service, which notifies creditors in case of credit card theft or loss.

Unless you are a credit history fanatic, you probably do not need to waste your money on a subscription to a credentials service. Since the same information will be reported on either a credentials-provided credit report or one you request on your own, it is likely to be cheaper just to get one on your own. While you should review your credit file once every two to three years, there is no real need for unlimited copies or instantaneous notice whenever a creditor runs a credit report on you.

You can also very easily create your own consumer financial profile by simply listing your positive credit information and submitting it along with your credit applications. However, don't be misled into thinking that you will be able to essentially rewrite your credit report through a consumer financial profile. Rather, a consumer financial profile is a separate file you create and give potential creditors access to.

The credit-reporting agency will still give inquiring creditors a copy of the credit file they normally maintain on you. If privacy is a concern, you should also be aware that credentials gives creditors easy access to all of the information you place in the file. Thus, if you subscribe to credentials and later experience repayment problems, creditors can use their credentials-provided information against you.

Credit Repair Companies

Be extremely cautious about the many private, *for-profit* credit repair companies that are springing up all over the country. Advertisements for so-called "credit doctor" services can usually be found in the Sunday classified section of most major newspapers. Typical ads read: "Get Out of Debt," "Credit Problems?—No Problem," "Credit Headaches?" "Bad Credit? " "Credit Profile Improvement Specialists," "Get Credit," "Come to the Credit Experts—We Erase Bad Credit," and "Credit Cleanup Guaranteed or Your Money Back."

Many of these services boldly advertise that you can "start living again " that they can restore your credit rating regardless of how many times you've been turned down for credit. They promise help, no matter how much you owe and even if you are past due everywhere. Some even claim they can remove delinquencies, liens, judgments, or bankruptcies from your credit report.

These agencies are usually expensive; fees of several hundred dollars are common. Prices range from as low as $75 to more than $2,000. Sizable initial deposits are sometimes required to "set up" an account. Some credit repair companies charge a percentage of your outstanding debt as their fee. Thus, if a credit doctor's fee is 12 percent of your debt, and you owe $5,000, the fee would total $600—an amount that could go a long way toward paying outstanding bills. As the result of a large number of consumer complaints, several states have enacted laws designed to stop abusive credit repair practices. In addition, the Federal Trade Commission routinely conducts investigations and brings law enforcement actions against unscrupulous credit repair practitioners. Congress is also considering legislation addressing credit repair company abuses.

Credit repair companies offer consumers nothing more than false hope. They prey on intimidated, exasperated, and vulnerable people by proffering the unrealistic prospect of a clean credit record. They take advantage of individuals desperate to appear creditworthy and improve their chances for obtaining credit. In actuality, there is very little likelihood that a credit repair company can change or remove *accurate* adverse information from a credit report.

Credit repair agencies may be successful in obtaining the removal or revision of *inaccurate or incomplete* information from a credit file. Nonetheless, there is no reason to pay through the nose for the credit repair agency to perform simple tasks that you can very easily accomplish yourself.

Instead of wasting your hard-earned money on the dubious services of a credit repair company, follow the suggestions in the preceding section, "Improving Your Credit Report." Following those few simple steps should assure the same or better results than you would probably get from a credit repair company, at considerably less cost.

Should you still decide to use the services of a credit repair company, make sure to get the following *in writing before you participate:*

- Information concerning your rights under the Fair Credit Reporting Act
- Full disclosure of the precise services the company will provide, a detailed listing of your obligations (if any),

itemization of all costs for services (including payment-due dates), and information concerning your right to cancellation
- Whether the company is required under state law to post a surety bond and the identity of its legal representative (so you can get your money back if the company closes)

CHAPTER 10

Special Credit Concerns

Women and Credit

Imagine yourself in the following situations:

• For several years Susan has used her husband's local hardware store charge card and faithfully paid the monthly bills. However, when she applied for a card in her own name, her application was rejected.

• After her husband died, Georgette was astonished that many of her creditors required her to reapply for credit cards she had held for years.

• After her divorce from Ralph, Gina moved across the country, resumed using her maiden name, and applied for a car loan. In spite of her past positive credit history as Ralph's wife, Gina's loan application was rejected because she had no credit history of her own.

• Peter and Sylvia had several joint obligations. When they got copies of their credit reports, all the joint obligations appeared on Peter's credit report; several were not reflected on Sylvia's credit report.

Even though Susan had been diligent in repayment activities on credit obligations for years, her efforts had created a stellar repayment history—for her husband! She had never developed a credit history in her own name. Georgette had relied on her husband's income when applying for her credit cards. When her creditors learned of his death, Georgette had to assure them she still had the financial resources to support her cards. While Gina had created a strong credit identity, when she moved and changed her name, her credit history was lost and did not follow her. Sylvia had attempted to create her own credit history through the establishment of joint obligations. However, some of her creditors had only reported these joint accounts in her husband's name.

The Need to Develop a Strong, Independent Credit Identity

Everyone should develop his or her own financial identity and try to assure a strong individual—independent—credit history.

If you have been or currently are married, you must be certain to develop a financial identity that is separate and apart from that of your spouse. In addition, a separate identity gives both spouses greater independence for managing day-to-day financial matters. A couple's financial security is enhanced by both spouses having their own financial identities. Such identities are also crucial in the event of divorce, death, or incapacity.

Establishing Credit in Your Own Name

If you have never held credit in your own name, you should make every effort to obtain credit in your own right as quickly as possible. To assist you, follow the advice in the "Borrowing for the First Time" section, which follows.

Make certain to apply for credit in your own name, using

your own Social Security number, and based on your own financial resources. If you and your spouse are Jane and John Doe, do not apply for credit as Mrs. John Doe. If you and your husband divorce and he subsequently remarries, there could be two Mrs. John Does. Thus, apply as either Jane Doe or Mrs. Jane Doe. When listing financial resources, do not list items that are held solely by your spouse. List your own income, financial resources, and any joint accounts for which you share responsibility. Be sure also to list any joint assets that you and your spouse may share.

Once you've obtained credit in your own name, keep your payments current. This will assure that you are building a strong, independent credit record for yourself.

Joint Obligations

If you and your spouse jointly hold credit obligations, these should appear on both of your credit reports (assuming the creditor reports to a credit reporting agency). This is because under a joint account relationship, you are both equally responsible for repayment of the obligation.

When applying for new joint credit accounts, make certain your name is indicated as above and that your financial resources, along with your spouse's, are considered by the creditor when reviewing your application. This should assure the reporting of the account under both your names. It also makes no difference who will be the primary user of the account, just so long as the account is held in both of your names.

The federal Equal Credit Opportunity Act (ECOA) entitles you to have any existing accounts (provided they were opened *after* June 1, 1977) that you use or for which you are liable listed on both your and your spouse's credit reports. Thus if a joint account appears on your husband's credit report but does not appear on yours, you have the right to have this account listed on your credit report. This can be done even without your spouse's permission.

To assure reporting in both names, send each of your joint creditors a letter similar to the following:

Dear Creditor:

My spouse and I share the following account with your firm:

_____.
(type of account, account number)

The following name appears on our most recent bill:

_____.

When reporting information to credit-reporting agencies, please make certain to report this account in both of the following names:

_____
(husband's name, Social Security number, joint or user status)

_____
(wife's name, Social Security number, joint or user status)

Our address is: _____
                    (street or mailing address)

                _____
                    (city, state, zip code)

Thank you for your prompt attention to this request.
Sincerely,

_____
(signature of either spouse)

If you and a spouse opened any joint accounts *before* June 1, 1977, these obligations may only appear on your husband's or former husband's credit report and may not be reflected on your credit report. If so, contact your creditors and ask them to report the obligations in both of your names. In addition, you might also contact the credit-reporting agency and request that information on these accounts be added to your file. You will probably be asked to verify your joint status on the account. If the credit-reporting agency is willing to include such information, you may be assessed a small fee for each item included. Under ECOA creditors are only required to dually report joint accounts opened after June 1, 1977.

Authorized User Status

Sometimes when credit is applied for in the husband's name based on his income, the wife may be listed as an authorized user on the account. Under such a setup, you may charge to the account or pay the bill, but your husband is primarily responsible for the account. This account may appear on your credit report. If it does, an authorized user status will probably be indicated.

While being an "authorized user" is not as good as holding credit in your own name, a favorable report on an obligation with your name listed as an authorized user should be viewed positively by potential creditors. However, be aware that if there are repayment problems on an account where you are listed as an authorized user, a negative report on the obligation will also appear on your credit report. The only way you can get such information deleted from your credit report is to prove that you did not use the account and were not responsible for the repayment problems.

Joint Assets

Make certain that any joint assets are held in both your name and your spouse's. Thus if you buy a house or farm, open bank accounts, invest in the stock market, and so on, be sure that both names appear as owners of the asset and/or that you have a right to survivorship. List such jointly held assets on any credit applications you may submit.

Credit Under Different Names

If you have ever held credit under a *different name* (maiden name, remarriage, divorce, name change), make certain your local credit-reporting agency lists these additional credit experiences under your *current name*. You might be able to get these additional obligations reported under your current name simply by requesting a copy of your credit report. On your request list all names along with the addresses where you lived under these names during the preceding five years. You should also contact your creditors directly and ask them to change the name on your accounts to reflect your new name.

Credit at Different Locations

Similarly, if you have moved and held credit at a different location, make sure the credit-reporting agency knows your previous addresses during the past five years. Then, if your accounts at previous addresses still do not appear on your credit report, you might consider contacting a credit-reporting agency that serves your previous addresses to obtain a copy of your credit report for each location. You can then submit a copy of these credit reports, along with your credit applications, to potential creditors for their consideration.

Avoid Credit Pitfalls

By following the steps outlined above, you should be able to create a strong credit history in your own right. However, be wary of the following pitfalls:

Do Not Rely on Your Spouse's Income to Get Credit. If you apply for your own credit card, do not rely on your husband's income as the sole basis for the credit extension. Instead, list your income and assets, along with any individual or joint obligations you may have. If you do not have enough resources to meet your creditor's income standards, get your husband or someone else to cosign your application. Then, once you have demonstrated your ability to make timely payments, you should be able to get credit in your own right.

A creditor may not cancel a credit obligation on learning of the loss of your spouse through death, divorce, or separation. However, if you currently have obligations that were based on your husband's income, your creditors—on learning of your changed marital status—may require you to reapply or update your application. While you should still be given access to the account while you are being reevaluated, it can be pretty upsetting to be forced to reapply for credit during a highly emotional period in which you may have diminished resources.

Remove Your Name from Joint Accounts in Cases of Separation or Divorce. If you and your spouse separate or divorce, protect yourself by removing your name from any joint accounts you may share. Send each of your joint creditors a letter indicating you and your husband are separated or divorced and that you will no longer be responsible for any *future* indebtedness incurred on the account. You will, of course, remain liable on *past* joint indebtedness. Your failure to remove your name from joint accounts may make you liable for your former spouse's future debts. And, if he encounters repayment problems later on, a negative credit report on the joint account may wind up on your credit report.

If you have a good repayment history on a joint obligation

and have sufficient income to meet your creditor's income standards, you should be able to get your own account with your former joint creditor.

Do Not Continue to Use Your Deceased Husband's Credit. Some widows may be tempted to continue to use their deceased husband's credit. This is awfully risky since the creditor will probably unilaterally cancel the account as soon as he or she learns of your spouse's death. If you keep the account current, the creditor may never have reason to suspect your spouse's death. However, your good repayment efforts will be reflected on your deceased husband's credit report, not your own.

In such cases, you should assume that the creditor will eventually learn of your spouse's death. You simply cannot base your financial well-being on such perilous circumstances. If you have sufficient financial resources, you should apply for credit in your own name. Of course, it is best to have obtained your own accounts and developed your own credit history during your husband's lifetime.

Special Credit Rules in Community Property States

If you live in Arizona, California, Idaho, Louisiana, Nevada, New Mexico, Texas, or Washington, you live in a community property state. Under community property law, creditors may consider your husband's credit history when you apply for an account in your own name. Thus, you have an added incentive in a community property state to assist your husband in maintaining a good credit history. Nevertheless, you should still make certain to develop a credit history of your own.

Borrowing for the First Time

Suppose you are a high school or college graduate whose efforts to obtain credit are repeatedly denied. Frustrated, you ask, "If it takes credit to get credit, how do I get started?"

Your dilemma rests with the credit-granting process. Creditors review your application and compare it to information contained in your credit report. This report provides the creditor with an independent means of assessing your creditworthiness. A problem arises if you do not have a credit history on file with a credit-reporting agency. Potential creditors have no independent way of either verifying information on your application or evaluating the risk you may pose to them. If you are borrowing for the first time, you may have trouble obtaining credit since this essential information does not exist for you.

If you do not have a credit history, you must immediately start building a strong one. A solid credit history will have far-reaching effects on your creditworthiness for years to come.

The following actions are recommended for developing a credit history. Feel free to utilize whichever actions you like. However, do not apply for a fistful of credit cards at once, since creditors might fear you are trying to obtain too much credit too quickly. Be pragmatic and restrained, and do not apply for more credit than you can realistically repay. Once you obtain a card, do not abuse it and do make prompt payments. Then, when you apply for another credit card or loan, use your good payment record with your original creditor as a stepping-stone for obtaining additional credit.

• Apply for a retail charge account (store or gasoline charge accounts) or a bank credit card (VISA, MasterCard,

Discover, or Choice). Determine the lowest possible credit limit on the account/card and request that amount as your credit limit. If you receive the account or card, be cautious. Keep charges to a minimum, and always make required payments in a timely manner.

• See if any organizations or groups you belong to (labor unions, associations, alumni organizations, professional membership groups, motoring clubs, or frequent-flyer programs) offer credit cards to their members. If one is offered, apply. Such cards may have fairly liberal credit criteria since they are offered on the basis of your affiliation with the organization. The card might also offer favorable terms, as the result of your organization's ability to negotiate the best possible deal for its members. Apply for the lowest line of credit available. If you get a card, use it sparingly and be judicious in your payments.

• Establish an ongoing relationship with a financial institution—bank, savings and loan, or credit union. This can be done by simply opening either a checking or savings account. Make sure not to overdraw on a checking account. The existence of a savings account will indicate financial responsibility. While having an account will not actually appear on your credit report, it indicates the establishment of a prudent money management practice.

• After you have established a relationship with a financial institution, apply for a loan. Request a small amount, with terms you can easily meet. Since you are a customer, the loan should be relatively easy to obtain. If your loan is approved, keep payments current.

• If you are applying for a car loan, the car will serve as collateral for the lender in the event you fail to pay. As a result a car loan is a secured loan, with the creditor retaining a security interest in the car. Since the creditor can always repossess if you fail to make payments, a car loan should be fairly easy to obtain. However, if you have no credit history, you may be asked to cough up a sizable down payment. Normal car loans finance only 80 percent of the car price, with the remaining 20 percent required as a down payment from the customer. If you have no credit history, you might expect a required down payment in excess of the normal 20 percent of the purchase price. However, if a car dealer is particularly anxious to sell you a car, you may find him or her willing to take the risk of extending you credit on basically the same terms as other customers. In addition, you might be able to benefit from the low interest rates occasionally offered by some dealers. Keep payments current if you get the car loan.

• In some instances, it may be necessary to obtain your first credit extension through the use of a family member, relative, or friend as a cosigner on your loan. This person becomes legally obligated to pay your indebtedness if you should fail to make the required payments. Since the cosigner is assuming ultimate responsibility for your debt, his or her credit history will be used when evaluating the creditworthiness of your loan request. Therefore, the cosigner has to be someone who has a good credit history and is financially responsible. However, the loan itself will be in your name and will be indicated on your credit report. If the loan is approved, you must make timely payments. Your failure to do so may trigger your cosigner's responsibility to pay.

Cosigning a Loan

Suppose a close friend or relative is having trouble getting a loan because some negative information appears on his or her credit report. Based on this, a potential creditor is unwilling to take a risk by extending credit. However, the creditor has indicated that the only way the loan can be obtained is to have a financially responsible person, with a good credit rating, cosign it. The creditor wants you to assume a risk he is not willing to undertake. Do you cosign or not?

By cosigning a loan, you are making a legal commitment to repay the full amount of the loan due, usually with late fees and collection costs, should the original borrower fail to make payments according to the terms of the loan agreement. In most states, if the original borrower misses or is late on a single payment, creditors can *immediately* look to you, the cosigner, for repayment. They do not even have to pursue the original debtor first.

Before you sign on the dotted line, consider the consequences. You should first realistically assess whether the person asking you to cosign is a financially responsible person. Will he or she make every effort to keep the loan current so your obligation to pay will not be triggered? What is the likelihood that you would be able to recoup your losses—from the original borrower—if you had to repay the loan? If you are considering cosigning for someone like a son or daughter who is trying to build a good credit history, are you in a position to assure payments are kept current?

Make certain you can afford to pay in the event of a default. If your repayment responsibilities are triggered and you fail to pay, it is the same thing as a default on obligations you hold in your own right. You could be sued. If the creditor wins the lawsuit, your wages may be garnished or your property taken to satisfy the judgment. A negative entry would probably appear on your credit report.

You should also consider whether your liability on this debt will discourage future creditors from extending credit to you, since they may view you as potentially overextended. If you pledge some of your property as security for the loan, be aware that you could lose this property in the event of default.

Should you decide to cosign, to protect yourself you should try to obtain a commitment from the creditor, in writing, that you be notified in cases of late or missed payments. This will allow you to be forewarned of your impending obligation to repay. Also ask the borrower to provide you with copies of all relevant documents concerning the loan for your records (since the creditor is probably not obligated to provide them). You might also see if the creditor would be willing to limit your liability on the obligation to the repayment of principal only, thereby saving yourself the cost of late fees or collection costs. Since some state laws provide additional protections to cosigners, you should determine whether such protections are available under your state's laws.

If you are considering cosigning a loan, the creditor is required to disclose to you most of the above information *before* you cosign the loan. These disclosures are required by Credit Practices Rules adopted by the federal regulatory agencies, which supervise creditor activities.

CHAPTER 11

Avoiding Future Credit Problems

Once you are clear of your credit problems, your experiences will have probably taught you how to plan carefully to avoid another financial crisis. To play it safe, be mindful of the following.

Developing New Financial Goals

When dealing with your financial problems, you no doubt established such financial goals as developing repayment plans with creditors and keeping current on payments. After you have seen yourself clear of these problems, you should develop new financial goals, including avoiding the use of credit, living on cash, and establishing savings practices.

Generally, your goal should be to move away from the debit side of consumer credit issues and toward the savings side. You will then be entering the exciting world of investments, which opens up delightful new opportunities and challenges.

Limiting Your Future Use of Credit

If you do not shun the use of credit for the time being, limit immediate credit use to no more than 10 percent of your annual take-home pay. Be fastidious in your repayment activities. If you are careful in your future use of credit, no future problems should be encountered.

Monitoring Credit and Spending Practices

Continually monitor your future credit and spending practices. Be on the lookout for credit danger signals, be careful not to exceed tolerable spending limits, and observe recommended spending guidelines. If you should discover a problem arising, deal with it promptly. Do not allow yourself to lapse into old behaviors.

Establishing Prudent Savings Practices

Since you have become accustomed to making regular monthly payments on your obligations, you should establish prudent savings practices. Continued payments can very easily be earmarked for a savings account. In addition, you have probably already adapted your life-style to living on a budget. To plan ahead for exigencies like unemployment, car and home repairs, medical expenses, a death in the family, or emergency travel expenses, strive to accumulate a savings nest egg. A minimum nest egg totaling three months' take-home pay is suggested; a six-month cushion is highly recommended.

Shop around for an account that gives you the highest possible rate of interest as well as quick access to your funds.

Avoid accounts with service charges and fees that may diminish the amount of interest you will earn.

An excellent resource in helping you select an account is *The Bank Book: How to Get the Most for Your Banking Dollars*, by Naphtali Hoffman and Stephen Brobeck. It is available in paperback for $5.95 from:

Consumer Federation of America
1424 16th Street, NW, Suite 604
Washington, DC 20036
(202)387–6121

Streamlining Your Financial Matters

Direct Deposits

If you have a bank account, you should consider having funds from checks you routinely receive (like paychecks, government assistance checks, social security checks) directly deposited into your account. The benefits of direct deposit include:

- Direct deposit is automatic; if you are sick, out of town, away from work, you still get paid on time
- Direct deposit will sometimes give you earlier access to funds than regular paychecks
- Direct deposit allows you to avoid long lines at the bank and increases your personal safety through your not having to carry around large amounts of cash
- Direct deposit may entitle you to a free or reduced-cost account with a financial institution

Automatic Bill Payments

You might also consider automatic bill payments to handle routine obligations like recurring car payments, loan repayments, mortgage payments. With automatic bill payments, funds are automatically debited from your bank account on the same date each month and applied to your outstanding loan balance. Make sure to include these payments in your bank account ledger and deduct the amount from your account balance.

Consider the following concerning automatic bill payments:

- Pursue automatic bill payments only if you are sure money will always be in your account on your payment date each month; if funds are not there, you will overdraft your account
- Automatic payments simplify bill paying; for those payments handled automatically, you won't have to write out and mail a check each month
- Prompt payment of your bill is assured through automatic payment; thus, you will avoid late payment penalties on automatic payment obligations
- Automatic payment may qualify you for a lower interest rate on a new loan since your financial institution's administrative costs are reduced through automatic payments

Using Your Success as a Basis for Dealing with Other Problems

Use your success in dealing with your credit problems as a stepping-stone toward the resolution of other nonfinancial problems. You will have proved you can take on a difficult task and emerge a victor. This experience should have demonstrated to you that there is hope for change in other areas of your life, and that you have the strength to deal with these matters. Apply the principles and experiences you have gained through dealing with your credit problems to other problems.

Helping Others Experiencing Credit Difficulty

Share your experiences, strength, and hope with others who may be going through credit difficulty. Your helping hand may be exactly what someone else needs when grappling with credit problems. Since you've already experienced the same or similar problems, others will probably benefit from your insights and suggestions.

Dealing with credit problems is a learning process. Not only do you learn how to handle specific problems but you also learn a little more about yourself—what your strengths, limitations, and vulnerabilities are. This knowledge should be invaluable to you as you approach future financial decisions, and it can serve as a basis for dealing with a host of other issues in your life.

If you've followed the above advice, you should be free of credit- and debt-related worries. Isn't it a good feeling to be rid of these problems? You should savor your success, move on, and turn your sights toward other areas for improvement in your life.

Good luck!

Appendix 1

How to Enforce Your Rights

You are entitled to access to information and specific rights under the federal consumer credit statutes (Fair Credit Reporting Act, Fair Credit Billing Act, Fair Debt Collection Practices Act, Truth-In-Lending Act, Fair Credit Card Disclosure Act, Equal Credit Opportunity Act, Electronic Funds Transfer Act). If you wish to enforce your rights under any of these statutes, your options are listed below.

Complain to Creditors and Credit-Reporting Agencies Directly. If you have a complaint against a creditor or a credit-reporting agency, you should first register your complaint with the establishment with which you have the complaint. Do not rely on a telephone conversation; put your complaint in writing. Also, do not rely on the decisions of subordinates; find out the name and address of an officer or the person in charge and send your complaint to that person. If it is a large organization and you are dissatisfied with the initial resolution of your dispute, make an appeal to the head of the department, the divisional manager, or the president of the company.

In your letter, make sure to present your version of the situation and why you feel a complaint is necessary. If you believe that a federal law or regulation has been violated, make it clear that you are aware of the law. Give the creditor or credit-reporting agency your preferred resolution of the problem, listing a couple of options that might also resolve the conflict. Say that you expect a prompt response (by a certain date, for example, within two weeks). If you have no reply by the deadline you have set, send a follow-up letter, call to check on the status of your complaint, or file a complaint with the appropriate federal regulatory agency. Keep a copy of the letter for your files and possible further use.

Complain to a Federal Regulatory Agency.   A complaint to a federal regulatory agency must also be in writing. When filing such a complaint, make sure to include the following information:

- Your name, address, and telephone number
- The name and address of the company you are complaining about
- Types of transactions and accounts involved in the complaint; give precise information, such as account numbers and the like
- Give details of the complaint, along with dates, company activities, your actions, company responses, and so on; substantiate your position with pertinent documents and copies of letters you mailed or received, if possible, give the names of the people with whom you discussed the matter, along with the dates of your interaction
- Sign and date your complaint letter

Since federal regulatory agencies are not responsible for resolving individual cases, do not expect them to intercede on your behalf once they receive your complaint. Your complaint will be grouped with other consumer complaints. These complaints might help the agency to determine if a pattern of practice exists (for example, a particular institution has a habit of discriminating against women). Your complaint, along with others, may alert the agency to a violation of a consumer credit statute.

If you have a complaint, ask the creditor or credit-reporting agency for the name and address of the federal regulatory agency that has jurisdiction over its activities. You can also determine the appropriate federal regulatory agency from the information provided below. Appendix I provides the national headquarters and regional office addresses to which to direct your complaint. You might complain to the regional office nearest you as well as the headquarters office. Also, mail a copy of the letter you send the federal regulatory agency to the institution you are complaining about. If the institution knows you are taking your complaint to a higher authority, it might be more willing to accommodate your request.

Sue in Federal Court. If you have a strong case and wish to pursue actions beyond those mentioned above, you should consult an attorney about possibly bringing suit in federal district court against the creditor or credit-reporting agency about which you feel aggrieved. You can usually either bring a suit in your own right or participate in a class-action suit. Federal law often limits the amounts of judicial awards under such suits.

You May Also Be Protected Under a State Law. Some states have enacted laws to protect their citizens concerning certain consumer financial transactions. If a state law assures the same protections and does not conflict with a federal law or regulation, the state law will usually apply. You should check to see if your state has enacted any laws that supplement the federal protections to which you are entitled. If so, you can either file a complaint with the appropriate state agency or possibly sue in a state court.

Type of Complaint	Where to Complain
Credit-reporting agency, retail or department store, finance or loan company, public utility company, state credit union, government-lending program, or travel and expense credit card company	Federal Trade Commission
Nationally chartered bank (*National* or *NA* will be part of the name)	Comptroller of the Currency
State-chartered bank, member of the Federal Reserve System, FDIC Insured (signs indicating either or both will appear on door or in lobby of bank)	Federal Reserve Board
State-chartered bank, FDIC insured but not a member of the Federal Reserve System	Federal Deposit Insurance Corporation
Federally chartered or insured savings and loan association	Office of Thrift Supervision U.S. Treasury Department
Federally chartered credit union	National Credit Union Administration

Federal Regulatory Agency Addresses

Federal Trade Commission

Office of Credit Practices
Bureau of Consumer Protection
FTC
Washington, DC 20580
(202) 326–3175

Regional Offices
Call or write to the Consumer Affairs Division at the following regional offices:

Atlanta Regional Office of the FTC
1718 Peachtree Street, NW, Room 1000
Atlanta, GA 30367
(404) 347–4836

Boston Regional Office of the FTC
10 Causeway Street, Room 1184
Boston, MA 02222–1073
(617) 565–7240

Chicago Regional Office of the FTC
55 East Monroe Street, Suite 1437
Chicago, IL 60603
(312) 353–4423

Cleveland Regional Office of the FTC
668 Euclid Street, Suite 520A
Cleveland, OH 44114
(216) 522–4210

Dallas Regional Office of the FTC
100 North Central Expressway, Suite 500
Dallas, TX 75201
(214) 767–5501

Denver Regional Office of the FTC
1405 Curtis Street, Suite 2900
Denver, CO 80202–2393
(303) 844–2271

Los Angeles Regional Office of the FTC
11000 Wilshire Boulevard
Los Angeles, CA 90024
(213) 209–7890

New York Regional Office of the FTC
2243 Federal Building
26 Federal Plaza
New York, NY 10278
(212) 264–1207

San Francisco Regional Office of the FTC
901 Market Street, Suite 570
San Francisco, CA 94103
(415) 995–5220

Seattle Regional Office of the FTC
2806 Federal Building
915 2nd Avenue
Seattle, WA 98174
(206) 442–4656

Federal Reserve Board

Division of Consumer and Community Affairs
Board of Governors of the Federal Reserve System
20th and C Streets, NW
Washington, DC 20551
(202) 452–3946

Regional Offices
Write to the Consumer Affairs Division at one of the following
regional offices:

Federal Reserve Bank of
  Boston
600 Atlantic Avenue
Boston, MA 02106
(617) 973–3000

Federal Reserve Bank of New
  York
Federal Reserve P.O. Station
New York, NY 10045
(212) 720–5000

Federal Reserve Bank of
  Philadelphia
PO Box 66
Philadelphia, PA 19105
(215) 574–6000

Federal Reserve Bank of
  Cleveland
PO Box 6837
Cleveland, OH 44101
(216) 579–2000

Federal Reserve Bank of
  Richmond
PO Box 27622
Richmond, VA 23201
(703) 697–8000

Federal Reserve Bank of
  Atlanta
PO Box 1731
Atlanta, GA 30301–1731
(404) 521–8500

Federal Reserve Bank of
  Chicago
PO Box 834
Chicago, IL 60690
(312) 322–5322

Federal Reserve Bank of St.
  Louis
PO Box 834
St. Louis, MO 63166
(314) 444–8444

Federal Reserve Bank of
Minneapolis
250 Marquette Avenue
Minneapolis, MN 55480
(612) 340–2345

Federal Reserve Bank of
Kansas City
925 Grand Avenue
Kansas City, MO 64198
(816) 881–2000

Federal Reserve Bank of
Dallas
Station K
Dallas, TX 75222
(214) 651–6111

Federal Reserve Bank of San
Francisco
PO Box 7702
San Francisco, CA 94120
(415) 974–2000

Comptroller of the Currency

Consumer Activities Division
OCC
490 L'Enfant Plaza, SW
Washington, DC 20219
(202) 287–4265

Regional Offices
Write to the Consumer Activities Division at the following regional
offices:

NE District, OCC
1114 Avenue of the Americas,
Suite 3900
New York, NY 10036
(212) 819–9860

SE District, OCC
Marquis Tower I, Suite 600
245 Peachtree Center Avenue,
NE
Atlanta, GA 30303
(404) 659–8855

Central District, OCC
1 Financial Place, Suite 2700
440 South LaSalle Street
Chicago, IL 60605
(312) 663–8000

Midwest District, OCC
2345 Grand Avenue, Suite
700
Kansas City, MO 64108
(816) 556–1800

SW District, OCC   Western District, OCC
1600 Lincoln Plaza   50 Fremont, Suite 3900
500 North Akard   San Francisco, CA 94105
Dallas, TX 75201–3394   (415) 545–5900
(214) 720–0656

Office of Thrift Supervision
U.S. Treasury Department

Office of Community Investment
Thrift Supervision Office, U.S. Treasury Department
1700 G. Street, NW
Fifth Floor
Washington, DC 20552
(202) 906–6237

Regional Offices
Write to the Consumer Affairs Division of one of the following regional offices:

Boston Regional Office   Atlanta Regional Office
PO Box 9106 GMS   PO Box 105565
Boston, MA 02205–9106   Atlanta, GA 30348
(617) 542–0150   (404) 888–3845

New York Regional Office   Cincinnati Regional Office
1 World Trade Center   PO Box 598
New York, NY 10048   Cincinnati, OH 45201
(212) 912–4657   (513) 852–7563

Pittsburgh Regional Office   Indianapolis Regional Office
1 Riverfront Center   PO Box 60
20 Stanwix Street   Indianapolis, IN 46206
Pittsburgh, PA 15222–4893   (317) 236–7113
(412) 288–3414

Chicago Regional Office
111 East Wacker Drive, Suite
800
Chicago, IL 60601
(312) 565–5740

Des Moines Regional Office
907 Walnut Street
Des Moines, IA 50309
(515) 243–4211

Dallas Regional Office
500 East John Carpenter
Freeway
PO Box 916026
Dallas, TX 75261
(214) 541–6865

Topeka Regional Office
PO Box 176
Topeka, KS 66601
(913) 233–0507, ext. 428

San Francisco Regional Office
PO Box 7948
San Francisco, CA 94120
(415) 393–1225

Seattle Regional Office
1501 4th Avenue
Seattle, WA 98101–1693
(206) 340–2460

National Credit Union Administration

Public Affairs Division
NCUA
1776 G Street, NW
Washington, DC 20006
(202) 682–9650

Regional Offices
Write to the Public Affairs Division at one of the following regional offices:

Region 1 Office of NCUA
9 Washington Square
Washington Avenue
Extension
Albany, NY 12205
(518) 472–4554

Region 2 Office of NCUA
1776 G Street, NW
Washington, DC 20006
(202) 682–1900

Region 3 Office of NCUA
7000 Central Park Way, Suite
  1600
Atlanta, GA 30328
(404) 396–4042

Region 4 Office of NCUA
300 Park Boulevard, Suite 155
Ithaca, IL 60143
(312) 250–6000

Region 5 Office of NCUA
4807 Spicewood Springs
  Road, Suite 5200
Austin, TX 78759
(512) 482–4500

Region 6 Office of NCUA
2300 Clayton Road, Suite
  1350
Concord, CA 94520
(415) 825–6125

Appendix 2

Consumer Credit Counseling Service Directory 1989

Alabama

Consumer Credit Counseling
  Service of Alabama, Inc.
217 South Court Street, Suite
  317
Montgomery, AL 36104
Malda W. Farmer, Executive
  Director
(205) 265–8545

Alaska

Consumer Credit Counseling
  Service of Alaska
208 East 4th Avenue
Anchorage, AK 99501
Myra Hollibaugh, Executive
  Director
(907) 279–6501

Arizona

Consumer Credit Counseling
  Service of Arizona
1930 West Peoria, #104
Phoenix, AZ 85029
John A. Erickson, President
(602) 870–9040

Branch Offices:
Flagstaff (602) 774–1484
Luke Air Force Base (602)
  870–9040
North Phoenix (602) 870–
  9040
Tempe (602) 968–2277

(Schedule appointments
  through Phoenix office)
In State: toll free (800) 338–
  3328

Tucson Family Debt
  Counselors
6135 East Grant Road
Tucson, AZ 85712
Raul Lopez, Executive
  Director
(602) 722–3328
Branch office:
South Tucson (602) 882–9966

Arkansas

Family Service Agency
Consumer Credit
Counseling Service
2700 North Willow Drive
PO Box 500
North Little Rock, AR 72115
Paul E. Blackstone, ACSW
Executive Director
(501) 758–1881

California

Consumer Credit Counseling
Service of the North Coast
850 G Street, Suite G
Arcata, CA 95521
Charles B. Riche, Executive
Director
(707) 822–8536

Consumer Credit Counselors
of Kern County
1508 18th Street, Suite 212
Bakersfield, CA 93301
Nancy Johnson, Executive
Director
(805) 324–9628

Consumer Credit Counselors
of Fresno, Inc.
2135 Fresno Street, Room 210
Fresno, CA 93721
Ray Willingham, Executive
Director
(209) 233–6221

Consumer Credit Counselors
of Los Angeles
1300 West Olympic, Room
304
Los Angeles, CA 90015
Gary Stroth, Executive
Director
(213) 386–7601

Branch offices:
Bell
Gardena
Inglewood
Lakewood
Pasadena
Redondo Beach
Van Nuys

(Schedule appointments
through Los Angeles
office)
(213) 386–7601

Consumer Credit
Counselors, Twin Cities
729 D Street
Marysville, CA 95901
Alice Valentini, Manager/
Counselor
(916) 743–1785

Consumer Credit Counselors
of East Bay (Oakland)
405–14th Street, Suite 1012
Financial Center Building
Oakland, CA 94612
R. F. Happ, Manager
(415) 832–7555

Branch offices:
Martinez
Valleio

(Schedule appointments
through Oakland office)
(415) 832–7555

Consumer Credit Counselors
of the North Valley
1670 Market Street
118 Downtown Mall
PO Box 4044
Redding, CA 96099
Phyllis Solberg, Executive
Director
(916) 244–9626

Consumer Credit Counselors
of Inland Empire
3679 Arlington Avenue,
Suite E
Riverside, CA 92506
Anthony Fostier, Executive
Director
(714) 781–0114

Branch offices:
Big Bear Lake
Indio
Palm Springs

(Schedule appointments
through Riverside office)
(714) 781–0114

Consumer Credit Counselors
of Sacramento, Inc.
2115 J Street, Suite 7
Sacramento, CA 95816

Lee A. Sweet, CCCC/CCCE
Executive Vice President
(916) 444–0740

Satellite offices:
Auburn
Fairfield
Roseville
Woodland

(Schedule appointments
through Sacramento office,
counseling only)
(916) 444–0740

Consumer Credit Counselors
of San Diego
3055 Rosecrans Place
PO Box 370130
San Diego, CA 92137–0130
Paul T. Greer, President
(619) 224–2922

Satellite office:
Vista

(Schedule appointments
through San Diego office)
(619) 224–2922

Consumer Credit Counselors
of San Francisco and the
Peninsula
(also serving Marin and
Sonoma Counties)
31 Geary Street
San Francisco, CA 94108
Cathy Pietruszewski,
Executive Director
(415) 788–0288, 788–0259

Branch office:
Santa Rosa (707) 527–9221
(also serves San Rafael)
Joann Mitchell, Manager

Satellite office:
Burlingame (415) 788–0288,
788–0259

Consumer Credit Counselors
of Orange County, Inc.
1616 East Fourth Street, Suite
130
Santa Ana, CA 92701–5189
Carl Lindquist, President
(714) 547–8281

Consumer Credit Counselors
of Santa Clara Valley, Inc.
1825 De La Cruz Boulevard,
Suite 8
Santa Clara, CA 95050
Marilynn Thain, Executive
Director
(408) 988–7881

Branch offices:
Fort Ord
Monterey
Salinas
Santa Cruz
Palo Alto

(Schedule appointments
through Santa Clara office)
(408) 988–7881

Consumer Credit Counselors
of Mid-Counties
4410 N. Pershing Avenue, C
Stockton, CA 95207

Irene Freeman, Executive
Manager
(209) 478–0782

Branch office:
Modesto (209) 522–1261

Consumer Credit Counselors
of Ventura County
3445 Telegraph Road, Suite
105
Ventura, CA 93003
Brad McClain, Executive
Director
(805) 644–1500

Branch offices:
Arroyo Grande (805) 481–
8173
Solvang
Thousand Oaks

(Schedule appointments
through Ventura office)
(805) 644–1500

Colorado

Consumer Credit Counseling
Service of Pikes Peak Area
3595 East Fountain
Boulevard, Suite AB2
Colorado Springs, CO 80910
Carolyn Hauswald, Executive
Director
(719) 596–6211

Consumer Credit Counseling Service of Greater Denver, Inc.
5250 Leetsdale Drive, Suite 205
PO Box 228800
Denver, CO 80222
Larry Smith, President
(303) 321–8988
(303) 792–DEBT (information line)

Satellite offices:
Arapahoe County (303) 792–DEBT
Aurora (303) 792–DEBT
Bear Valley (303) 792–DEBT
Boulder (303) 792–DEBT
Downtown Denver (303) 792–DEBT
Grand Junction (303) 792–DEBT
Lakewood (303) 792–DEBT
Littleton (303) 792–DEBT
Lowry Air Force Base (303) 792–DEBT
Westminster (303) 792–DEBT

Money Management Counseling Service
222 West Laurel Street
Ft. Collins, CO 80521
Kathleen C. Green, Coordinator
(303) 484–7520

Satellite office:
Loveland

(Schedule appointments through Fort Collins office)
(303) 484–7520

Connecticut

Consumer Credit Counseling Service of Connecticut
151 New Park Avenue
Hartford, CT 06106
Beverly Tuttle, President
(203) 233–4471

Branch offices:
New Haven (203) 287–1209
Norwalk (203) 855–9594

Satellite offices:
U.S. Submarine Base, Groton (military only)
(203) 449–3383
Waterbury (203) 597–8917

Delaware

Dover (302) 674–4960
(Branch of CCCS, MD)

Northern Delaware, refer to Philadelphia, PA
(215) 563–5665

Southern Delaware, refer to Elkton, MD
(301) 392–5428

District of Columbia

Consumer Credit Counseling
Service of Greater
Washington, Inc.
(Branch of CCCS Rockville,
MD)
1120 G Street, NW, Suite
B175
Washington, DC 20005
Joanne Kerstetter, Executive
Director
Betty Matthews, Branch
Director
(202) 638–6996

Florida

Family Counseling Service
(CCCS Division)
1639 Atlantic Boulevard,
Suite 101
Jacksonville, FL 32207
Dawn Lockhart, Program
Director
(904) 396–4846

Branch office:
Bld. 214, 3201 Air Base
Group/FS
Eglin AFB, FL 32542–5000
(904) 882–4489

Satellite offices:
Jacksonville Beach (904) 246–
6539
Orange Park (904) 269–6679

Consumer Credit Counseling
Service of Pinellas County,
Inc.
801 West Bay Drive, Suite 313
SE Bank Building
Largo, FL 34640
Patricia Nurse, Executive
Director
(813) 585–0099

Branch office:
St. Petersburg (813) 585–0099

(Schedule appointments
through Largo office)
(813) 585–0099

Consumer Credit Counseling
Service of South Florida,
Inc.
13014 NE 8th Avenue
North Miami, FL 33161
Andrew J. McGehee,
Executive Director
(305) 893–5225

Branch offices:
Cutler Ridge (305) 233–2480
Fort Lauderdale (305) 765–
0502

Consumer Credit Counseling
Service of Marion County,
Inc.
PO Box 4110
Ocala, FL 32678
Richard E. Tuman, Executive
Director
(904) 694–2188, 694–2189

Consumer Credit Counseling Service of Central Florida, Inc.
1900 North Mills Avenue, Suite 5
Orlando, FL 32803
George C. Reed, Executive Director
(407) 896–2463, 896–2464, 896–2465

Branch offices:
Altamonte Springs (407) 339–6111
Daytona Beach (904) 761–5414
Lakeland (813) 644–9860
Naval Training Center (407) 646–4617

Satellite office:
Deltona (407) 574–3835 (Wednesday only)

Consumer Credit Counseling Service of West Florida, Inc.
2 North Palafox Street, Suite 221
PO Box 943
Pensacola, FL 32594
Doris J. Purser, Executive Director
(904) 434–0268

Satellite office:
Naval Training Center, Pensacola
(904) 452–6497

Consumer Credit Counseling Service of Brevard
(Division of Family Counseling Center)
220 Coral Sands Drive, Suite 1
PO Box 63
Rockledge, FL 32955
Robert A. Caldwell, ACSW President and CEO
Sidney T. Brooks, MSW Executive Director
(407) 632–5792

Branch office (client/creditor inquiry):
Melbourne (407) 259–1070

Satellite office:
Titusville (407) 269–7273

Consumer Credit Counseling Service of the Tampa Bay Area, Inc.
4265 Henderson Boulevard
Tampa, FL 33629
John C. McLaughlin, President and CEO
(813) 289–8923

Branch office:
Bradenton/Sarasota (813) 746–4476

Consumer Credit Counseling Service of Palm Beach County, Inc.
224 Datura Street, Suite 205
West Palm Beach, FL 33401
Dorothy G. Kunze, Executive Director
(407) 655–0885, 655–6433

Satellite offices:
Boca Raton East/West (407)
243–0102
Port St. Lucie (407) 879–0998
Stuart (407) 283–3188

Georgia

Consumer Credit Counseling
Service of Greater Atlanta,
Inc.
100 Edgewood Avenue, NE,
Suite 810
Atlanta, GA 30303
Fred R. Tonney, President
and CEO
(404) 527–7630

Branch offices:
Clayton County (404) 994–
0211
Cobb County (404) 977–3955
Gwinnett County (404) 441–
1952

Consumer Credit Counseling
Service
(a division of Family
Counseling Center)
102 7th Street
PO Box 1825
Columbus, GA 31902
Linda Smith, Division
Coordinator
(404) 327–3238

Consumer Credit Counseling
Service of Middle Georgia,
Inc.
654 First Street, Suite 5
PO Box 31
Macon, GA 31202
William P. Boisclair,
Executive Director
(912) 745–6197

Branch office:
Warner Robins (912) 922–
1141

Consumer Credit Counseling
Service of the Savannah
Area, Inc.
15 East Montgomery
Crossroads, Suites 1 and 2
Savannah, GA 31499
Frank Maceyko, Executive
Director
(912) 927–HELP

Hawaii

Consumer Credit Counseling
Service of Hawaii
1414 Colburn Street, Suite
202
Honolulu, HI 96817
Michael Haxton, Director
(808) 841–7516

Idaho

Consumer Credit Counseling
Service of Idaho, Inc.
6068 Emerald
PO Box 9264
Boise, ID 83703
Shirley A. Treharne,
Manager
(208) 375–8140

Branch office:
Nampa (208) 467–2927

Consumer Credit Counseling
Service of Northern Idaho,
Inc.
307 19th Street
Lewiston, ID 83501
Sheryl L. Choate, Executive
Director
(208) 746–0127

Consumer Credit Counseling
Service of Magic Valley
219 5th Avenue
PO Box 1085
Twin Falls, ID 83301
Pat Richards, Executive
Director
(208) 733–0586

Illinois

Family Counseling Service
122 West Downer Place
Aurora, IL 60506

Karl Flodstrom, Program
Director
(312) 844–3327

Family Counseling Center
720 West Chestnut Street
Bloomington, IL 61701
Jo Stephen Major, Executive
Director
(309) 828–4343

Consumer Credit Counseling
Services United Charities
14 East Jackson Boulevard
Chicago, IL 60604
Janice Tave, Director
(312) 461–0800

Branch offices:
Calumet Center (312) 264–
3010
Family and Mental Health
Services/Southwest (312)
448–5700
Loop Center (312) 939–1300
Midway Center (312) 436–
2400
Murdock Center (312) 829–
9327
Parkside Center (312) 282–
9535
South Chicago Center (312)
221–5141

Satellite office:
Northwest Suburban Office
(312) 939–1300

Consumer Credit Counseling
Service of Central Illinois
363 South Main Street, Suite
205
Decatur, IL 62523
Dr. Lynn S. Miller, Director
(217) 425–0654

Family Service Association of
Greater Elgin Area
Consumer Credit Counseling
Service
22 South Spring Street
Elgin, IL 60120
Catherine M. Williams,
Program Director
(312) 931–1260

Branch offices:
Dundee
Streamwood
(Schedule appointments
through Elgin office)
(312) 931–1260

Consumer Credit Counseling
Service of Evanston and
Skokie Valley
1114 Church Street
Evanston, IL 60201
John Buckley, Executive
Director
(312) 328–2404

Consumer Credit Counseling
Service of Greater
Chicago, Inc.
6525 West North Avenue,
Suite 203

Oak Park, IL 60302
Jerry Lewis, President
(312) 386–6600

Central Illinois Credit
Counseling Service, Inc.
1005 First National Bank
Building
Peoria, IL 61602
James P. Carr, Executive
Director
(309) 676–2941

Consumer Credit Counseling
Service of Springfield
1021 South Fourth Street
Springfield, IL 62703
Ron Peters, Director
(217) 523–3621

Consumer Credit Counseling
Service of Lake County
(Division of Catholic
Charities)
1 North Genesee, Suite 203
Waukegan, IL 60085
Vara Aiyappa, Director
(312) 249–3500

Family Service Association of
Dupage Budget
Counseling/Debt
Management
402 West Liberty Drive
Wheaton, IL 60187
Trevor Head, Director
(312) 682–1802

Satellite office:
Woodridge (312) 682–1802

Consumer Credit Counseling
Service of McHenry
County, Inc.
PO Box 746
Woodstock, IL 60098
Tom Nigbor, Executive
Director
(815) 338–5757

Indiana

Consumer Credit Counseling
Service
(Division of Family
Counseling Service of
Elkhart County)
101 East Hively Avenue
Elkhart, IN 46517
Anne Miller, Manager
(219) 295–6596

Consumer Credit Counseling
Service of Tri-State, Inc.
715 First Avenue, Suite 31
PO Box 4783
Evansville, IN 47724
Connie O. Russell, Executive
Director
(812) 422–1108

Consumer Credit Counseling
Service of Northeastern
Indiana
345 West Wayne Street
PO Box 11403

Fort Wayne, IN 46858
Thomas E. Hufford,
Executive Director
(219) 422–3806

Satellite office:
Warsaw (800) 552–3650 (in
Indiana)
(219) 422–4877 (all others)

Consumer Credit Counseling
Service of Northwest
Indiana, Inc.
3660 Grant Street, Suite 5
Gary, IN 46408
Barbara L. Bibb, Executive
Director
(219) 980–4800

Consumer Credit Counseling
Service of Central Indiana,
Inc.
615 North Alabama Street
Indianapolis, IN 46204
Marcele E. Everest, Executive
Director
(317) 632–4501

Family & Children's Services,
Inc.
CCCS Division
1411 Lincoln Way West
Mishawaka, IN 46544
Rosemary Moehle, CCCS
Coordinator
(219) 259–5666

Iowa

Family Service Agency—
Consumer Credit
Counseling
1330 1st Avenue, NE
Cedar Rapids, IA 52402
Scott Shook, Director
(319) 398–3574

Consumer Credit Counseling
Service of Des Moines
5515 Southeast 14th Street
Des Moines, IA 50320
Carl Coates, President
(515) 287–6428

Consumer Credit Counseling
Service
206 6th Street
Sioux City, IA 51101
Mike Ford, Counselor
(712) 252–1861

Consumer Credit Counseling
Service of Northeastern
Iowa, Inc.
438 Western Avenue
Waterloo, IA 50701
Karen Atwood, Executive
Director
(319) 234–0661

Kansas

Consumer Credit Counseling
Service, Inc.
122 North Santa Fe, Suite A
Salina, KS 67401
Ruth Self, Executive Director
(913) 827–6731

Branch office:
Wichita
Sharon Funke, Office
Manager/Counselor
(316) 266–8322

Consumer Credit Counseling
Service
Housing and Credit
Counseling, Inc.
1195 Southwest Buchanan,
Suite 203
Topeka, KS 66604
Karen Hiller, Executive
Director
(913) 234–0217

Satellite office:
Lawrence

(Schedule appointments
through Topeka office)
(913) 234–0217

Kentucky

Florence, Kentucky

(Schedule apointments
   through Cincinnati, Ohio,
   office)
(513) 651–0111

Louisiana

Family Debt Counselors of
   Greater Baton Rouge
615 Chevelle Court
Baton Rouge, LA 70806
(504) 927–4274
E. D. Sledge, President and
   CEO

Branch office:
Consumer Credit Counseling
   Service of Acadiana
615 South College Drive
Lafayette, LA 70503
(318) 232–IOWE
Lisa Duplechain, Manager

Consumer Credit Counseling
   Service of Greater New
   Orleans, Inc.
1539 Jackson Avenue, Room
   201
New Orleans, LA 70130
Vern Svendson, President
   and CEO
(504) 529–2396

Branch office:
Slidell (504) 641–4158

Maine

Credit Counseling Centers,
   Inc.
991 Forest Avenue
PO Box 1021
Portland, ME 04104
G. ("Rick") Dobson, Jr.,
   Executive Director
(207) 878–2874

Satellite offices:
Augusta
Bangor
Bath
Lewiston

(Schedule appointments toll
   free: [800] 882–CCCS)

Maryland

Consumer Credit Counseling
   Service of Maryland, Inc.
Fayette Street & Luzerne
   Avenue
Bradford Federal Building,
   2nd Floor
Baltimore, MD 21224
Victor L. Boehm, President
(301) 732–3604

Branch offices:
Bel Air (301) 838–6112
Dover, DE (302) 674–4960
Elkton (301) 392–5428
Hagerstown (301) 733–5810
Laurel (301) 498–9400
Salisbury (301) 742–4422

Satellite office:
Westminster (301) 848–5758

Consumer Credit Counseling
   Service of Southeast
   Maryland, Inc.

Branch office:
Forestville, MD
(301) 420–4182

Consumer Credit Counseling
   and Educational Service of
   Greater Washington, Inc.
11426 Rockville Pike, Suite
   105
Rockville, MD 20852
Joanne Kerstetter, Executive
   Director
(301) 231–5833

Branch office:
Frederick (301) 831–4636

Mel R. Stiller, Executive
   Director
(617) 426–6644

Satellite offices:
Brockton (617) 426–6644
Worcester (508) 795–1444

Pioneer Valley Consumer
   Credit Counseling Service,
   Inc.
293 Bridge Street, Suite 221
PO Box 171
Springfield, MA 01101
Robin Walker, Executive
   Director
(413) 788–6106

Satellite offices:
Northampton
Southbridge

(Schedule appointments
   through Springfield office)
(413) 788–6106

Michigan

no service

Massachusetts

Consumer Credit Counseling
   Service of Eastern
   Massachusetts, Inc.
8 Winter Street, Suite 1210
Boston, MA 02108

Minnesota

Consumer Credit Counseling
Service of Duluth
(Division of Lutheran Social
Services of Minnesota)
424 West Superior Street
600 Ordean Building
Duluth, MN 55802
Jeanne H. Sampson,
Financial Consulting
Coordinator
(218) 726–4767

Branch offices:
Mankato (507) 625–7660
Willmar (612) 235–5411

Consumer Credit Counseling
Service of Minnesota, Inc.
1111 3rd Avenue South, Suite
360
Minneapolis, MN 55404
Wayne B. Wensley, President
(512) 349–6953

Branch offices:
Rochester (507) 281–4552
St. Cloud (701) 235–3328
(call collect)
(Branch of the Village Family
Service Center, Fargo, ND)

Family Service of St. Croix Area
CCCS Division
216 West Myrtle Street
Stillwater, MN 55082
(612) 439–4840
Sandra Shearer, Executive
Director

Mississippi

no service

Missouri

Consumer Credit Counseling
Service
(Division of Job Center)
19 East Walnut Street, Suite E
Columbia, MO 65203
Gladys Anderson, Executive
Director
(314) 443–0303

Consumer Credit Counseling
Service of Greater Kansas
City, Inc.
3435 Broadway, Suite 203
Kansas City, MO 64111
Nancy Nauser, Executive
Director
(816) 753–0535

Satellite offices:
Gladstone
Independence
Kansas City, KS
Overland Park

(Schedule appointments
through Kansas City, MO,
office)
(816) 753–0535

Consumer Credit Counseling
Service of Metropolitan St.
Louis, Inc.
1425 Hampton Avenue
St. Louis, MO 63139-8901
C. Philip Johnston, Executive
Director
(314) 647-9004

Branch office:
St. Charles (314) 946-9535

Consumer Credit Counseling
Service of Springfield,
Missouri
300 South Jefferson, Suite
510
Springfield, MO 65805
Wendell T. Gregory, Director
(417) 862-5139

Montana

Consumer Credit Counseling
Service of Billings,
Montana
2160 Central, Suite 4
Billings, MT 59102
Kathy Ruegamer, Executive
Director
(406) 656-3172

Consumer Credit Counseling
Service of Cascade County
1323 9th Avenue South
PO Box 2343
Great Falls, MT 59403
Duane Delphy, President
(406) 761-8721

Toll free in Montana: (800)
537-0872

Branch office:
Helena (406) 443-1774

Nebraska

Consumer Credit Counseling
Service of Nebraska, Inc.
PO Box 31002
Omaha, NE 68131
Donald A. Leu, Jr., President
(402) 345-3110

Branch office:
Lincoln (402) 467-5456

Nevada

Consumer Credit Counseling
Service of Las Vegas
3650 South Decatur, Suite 18
Las Vegas, NV 89103
Michele Johnson, Executive
Director
(702) 364-0344
Toll free (800) 451-4505
(Nevada residents only)

New Hampshire

Consumer Credit Counseling
Service of New Hampshire
and Vermont
Administrative Office
8 Union Street
PO Box 676
Concord, NH 03302
Patricia Muzzey, Executive
Director
(603) 224–6593

Branch office:
Manchester (800) 852–3385

Satellite offices:
Keene
Laconia
Nashua
Peterborough

(Schedule appointments
through Concord office)
(800) 852–3385

New Jersey

Consumer Credit Counseling
Service of New Jersey, Inc.
76 Mount Kemble Avenue
Morristown, NJ 07960
Robert Allister, Executive
Director
(201) 267–4324

Mailing address:
PO Box 97C
Convent Station, NJ 07961

Branch office:
East Orange (201) 267–4324

New Mexico

Consumer Credit Counseling
Service of Albuquerque,
Inc.
5318 Menual, NE
Albuquerque, NM 87110–
3195
Helen Casey, Executive
Director
(505) 884–6601

Satellite office:
Kirtland Air Force Base
Family Support Center (505)
846–0751
Wednesday A.M.
appointments only

New York

Consumer Credit Counseling
Service of Buffalo, Inc.
43 Court Street
730 Convention Tower
Buffalo, NY 14202
John Y. Pax, Executive
Director
(716) 854–1710

Budget & Credit Counseling
Services, Inc.
115 East 23rd Street, 11th
Floor
New York, NY 10010
Luther R. Gatling, President
(212) 677–3066, 505–2430

Satellite office:
White Plains (914) 285–5972

Consumer Credit Counseling
Service of Rochester, Inc.
50 Chestnut Plaza
Rochester, NY 14604
Charles Foster, Executive
Director
(716) 546–3440

Consumer Credit Counseling
Service of Central New
York, Inc.
120 East Washington Street
1006 University Building
Syracuse, NY 13202
Sharon Patchett, Executive
Director
(315) 474–6026

Branch offices:
Binghamton (607) 772–1195
Utica (315) 797–5366

Satellite offices:
Fort Drum (315) 772–6894
Fulton (315) 598–3980
Griffiss Air Force Base
(315) 330–1110, × 3121

North Carolina

Consumer Credit Counseling
Service of Western North
Carolina, Inc.
50 South French Broad
Avenue, Suite 122
Asheville, NC 28801
Craig Laroche, Executive
Director
(704) 255–5166

Branch offices:
Brevard
Hendersonville
(Schedule appointments
through Asheville office)
(704) 255–5166

Consumer Credit Counseling
Service
(A division of United Family
Services)
301 South Brevard Street
Charlotte, NC 28202
Barbara Robinson,
Coordinator
(704) 332–4191

Branch office:
Union County (704) 283–1539

Consumer Credit Counseling
Service of Fayetteville
118 Gillespie Street
PO Box 272
Fayetteville, NC 28302
Kenneth G. Smith, Executive
Director
(919) 323–3192

Consumer Credit Counseling
Service of Gaston County
(A division of Family Service,
Inc.)
214 East Franklin Boulevard
Gastonia, NC 28052
Dewey T. Matherly, ACSW
Executive Director
(704) 864–7704

Branch office:
Shelby (704) 481–9419

Consumer Credit Counseling
Service of Guilford County
1301 North Elm Street
Greensboro, NC 27401
M. Edward Roach, Program
Director
Janet Payne, Senior
Counselor
(919) 373–1511

Consumer Credit Counseling
Service
17 Highway 64–70 SE
Hickory, NC 28602
Floyd J. Tucker, Program
Director
(704) 322–7161

Consumer Credit Counseling
(A division of Family
Services of Wake County,
Inc.)
PO Box 11665
Raleigh, NC 27604–0665
DeFrancia L. Scott, Director
(919) 821–1770

Consumer Credit Counseling
Service Family Services
2841 Carolina Beach Road
PO Box 944
Wilmington, NC 28402–0944
Teresa Morgan, Program
Director
(919) 799–8734

Consumer Credit Counseling
Service of Forsyth County,
Inc.
926 Brookstown Avenue
Winston-Salem, NC 27101–
3625
Z. Gray Jackson, Executive
Director
(919) 725–1958

Satellite office:
Lexington (704) 246–4814

North Dakota

The Village Family Service
Center
PO Box 7398
Fargo, ND 58109
Mark Carman, CCC
Director
(701) 235–3328

Branch offices:
Bismark (701) 255–3328
Grand Forks (701) 746–4584
Minot (701) 852–3328
St. Cloud, MN (701) 235–
3328
(Call collect)
Williston (800) 732–4475

(Schedule appointments
through Fargo office)
(701) 235–3328

Ohio

Family Services of Summit
County
CCCS Division
212 East Exchange Street
Akron, OH 44304
Robert P. Labbe, ACSW
Executive Director
Jeffrey N. James, Director
CCCS
(216) 376–9494
TTY for Deaf: (216) 376–9351

Consumer Credit Counseling
Service of Ashtabula
County
(Division of Catholic Service
League)
4436 Main Avenue
PO Box 1338
Ashtabula, OH 44004
Joan Sawyers, Director
(216) 992–2121

Consumer Credit Counseling
Service of Stark County,
Inc.
800 Market Avenue North
McKinley Centre
Canton, OH 44702
Kelli Baxter, Executive
Director
(216) 455–8118

Consumer Credit Counseling
Service
(A division of Family Service
of the Cincinnati Area)
205 West 4th Street, 2nd Floor
Textile Building
Cincinnati, OH 45202
Bernard J. Kaiser, Program
Director
(513) 651–0111

Branch office:
Florence, KY
(Schedule appointments
through Cincinnati office)
(513) 651–0111

Consumer Credit Counseling
Service of Northeastern
Ohio
509 Euclid Avenue, Suite 300
Cleveland, OH 44114
William DeVries, President/
Director
(216) 781–8624 (Cleveland
residents)
(800) 621–8261 (remainder of
Ohio)

Satellite offices:
Chardon
Elyria
Mentor
Parma
(Schedule appointments
through Cleveland office)
(216) 781–8624 (Cleveland
residents)
(800) 621–8261 (remainder of
Ohio)

Consumer Credit Counseling
Service of Central Ohio, Inc.
697 East Broad Street
Columbus, OH 43215
Paul B. Eberts, President and
CEO
(614) 464–2227

Branch offices:
Chillicothe (614) 464–2227
Delaware (614) 464–2227
Lancaster (614) 464–2227
Mansfield (419) 526–2770
Marion (614) 464–2227

Lutheran Social Services
CCCS Department
3304 North Main Street
PO Box 506
Dayton, OH 45405
Robert F. Libecap, Program
Manager
(513) 278–9617

Satellite offices:
Sidney (513) 492–1953
Springfield (513) 325–2898

Consumer Credit Counseling
Service, Family Service of
Butler County
111 Buckeye Street
Hamilton, OH 45011
Steve Lieurance, Program
Director
(513) 868–9220, 868–3245

Satellite office:
Lebanon (513) 932–6301
(513) 677–6100 Cincinnati
line toll free

Consumer Credit Counseling
Service of Portage County
302 North Depeyster
Kent, OH 44240
Mary Sites, Coordinator
(216) 678–4782

Consumer Credit Counseling
Service
(Division of Regional Family
Counseling, Inc.)
616 South Collett Street
Lima, OH 45805
Richard L. Acton, Executive
Director
(419) 227–9202

Consumer Credit Counseling
Service of Columbiana
County
966½ North Market Street
PO Box 413
Lisbon, OH 44432
Donna Beiling, Program
Director
(216) 424–7991

Consumer Credit Counseling
Service, Family
Counseling Service
126 West Church Street
Newark, OH 43055
Mary Green, Program
Manager
(614) 349–7051

Satellite office:
Mt. Vernon (614) 349–7051

Family Service CCCS of the
Upper Ohio Valley
(Branch of Family Service
Association, Wheeling,
West Virginia)
Steubenville, OH
Lonnie Wineman, Executive
Vice President
Shelly Meadows, CCCS
Director
(614) 283–4763

Consumer Credit Counseling
Program
1704 North Road, SE
Heaton Square
Warren, OH 44484
Nancy Gray, Coordinator
(216) 856–2907

Children's and Family Service
CCCS Division
535 Marmion Avenue
Youngstown, OH 44502
Kathy Virgallito, Program
Director
(216) 782–9113

Consumer Credit Counseling
Service of Muskingum
Valley
712 Market Street
Zanesville, OH 43701
Joanne Winland, Executive
Director
(614) 454–6909

Oklahoma

Consumer Credit Counseling
Service of Central
Oklahoma, Inc.
2519 Northwest 23rd
PO Box 75405
Oklahoma City, OK 73147
Gloria E. Kelley, Executive
Director
(405) 947–6631

Branch offices:
Lawton (405) 357–3932
Norman (405) 321–5731

Satellite offices:
Enid (405) 237–3230
Tinker Air Force Base (405)
739–2417, 739–2747

Credit Counseling Centers of
Oklahoma, Inc.
2140 South Harvard
PO Box 4450
Tulsa, OK 74159
Victor R. Schock, Director
(918) 744–5611

Satellite offices:
Bixby (918) 744–5611
Broken Arrow (918) 744–5611
Sapulpa (918) 224–8412

Oregon

Consumer Credit Counseling Service of Linn-Benton, Inc.
201 West First
PO Box 1006
Albany, OR 97321
Jan Amling, Executive Director
(503) 926–5843

Consumer Credit Counseling Service of Central Oregon, Inc.
1900 Northeast Division Street, Suite 205

Mailing address:
PO Box 5578
Bend, OR 97708
Barbara Preble, Executive Director
(503) 389–6181

Satellite offices:
Madras
Prineville

(Schedule appointments through Bend office)
(503) 389–6181

Consumer Credit Counseling Service of Lane County, Inc.
1601 B, Oak Street
Eugene, OR 97401
Roberta Dubois, Executive Director
(503) 342–4459

Consumer Credit Counseling Service of Southern Oregon, Inc.
820 Crater Lake Avenue, 206
Medford, OR 97504
Jan Safley, Director
(503) 779–2273

Satellite office:
Klamath Falls (503) 883–8118

Consumer Credit Counseling Service of Coos-Curry, Inc.
Pony Village Mall, Suite 17A
North Bend, OR 97459
Deborah L. Graham, Executive Director
(503) 756–4008

Consumer Credit Counseling Service Umatilla County, Inc.
17 Southwest Frazer, Suite 324
PO Box 582
Pendleton, OR 97801
John A. Amort, President
(503) 276–3856

Consumer Credit Counseling Service of Oregon, Inc.
3633 Southeast 35th Place
PO Box 42155
Portland, OR 97242
Lawrence Winthrop, President
(503) 232–8139

Douglas Consumer Credit
   Counseling Service
PO Box 1011
Roseburg, OR 97470
Linda Smith, Executive
   Director
(503) 673-3104

Consumer Credit Counseling
   Service of Mid-Willamette
   Valley, Inc.
1900 Hines Street, SE 100
PO Box 13609
Salem, OR 97309
Frank Lackey, Executive
   Director
(503) 581-7301

Pennsylvania

Consumer Credit Counseling
   Service of Lehigh Valley,
   Inc.
1031 Linden Street
Allentown, PA 18102
Albert J. Kotch, Executive
   Director
(215) 821-4011

Branch offices:
Pen Argel
Reading
(Schedule appointments
   through Allentown
   office)
(215) 821-4011

Consumer Credit Counseling
   Division Family Services
670 West 36th
Erie, PA 16508
James R. Fuller, Coordinator
(814) 454-6478

Tabor Community Services
CCCS Division
320 South Duke Street
Lancaster, PA 17602
Nevin Horst, Executive
   Director
(717) 397-5182

Consumer Credit Counseling
   Service of Delaware Valley
(Also serving southern New
   Jersey and Delaware)
1211 Chestnut Street, Suite
   411
Philadelphia, PA 19107
Thomas A. O'Neill,
   Executive Director
(215) 563-5665

Satellite office:
West Chester (215) 563-5665

Consumer Credit Counseling
   Service of Western
   Pennsylvania, Inc.
309 Smithfield Street, Suite
   2000
Pittsburgh, PA 15222
Jack R. Onorad, President
(412) 471-7584

Branch offices:
Blair County (814) 696–3546
Greensburg (412) 838–1290
New Castle (412) 652–8074

Satellite office:
Aliquippa (412) 652–8074

Consumer Credit Counseling
Service of Northeastern
Pennsylvania, Inc.
129 North Washington
Avenue
401 Connell Building
PO Box 168
Scranton, PA 18501
Michael A. Elick, Executive
Director
(717) 342–1072, 655–9527

Satellite offices:
East Stroudsburg
Shamokin
Wilkes-Barre
Williamsport

(Schedule appointments
through Scranton office)
(717) 342–1072, 655–9527

Rhode Island

Consumer Credit Counseling
Division, Rhode Island
Consumers' Council
365 Broadway
Providence, RI 02909
Edwin Palumbo, Executive
Director
(401) 277–2764

South Carolina

Consumer Credit Counseling
Service of Greater
Charleston, SC
3005 West Montague, Suite F
Charleston, SC 29418
Donald Buckland, Director
(803) 747–3616

Family Service Center
1800 Main Street
PO Box 7876
Columbia, SC 29202
L. Russell Rawls, Jr.,
President and CEO
M. Susie Irvine, Director,
CCCS
(803) 733–5450, 733–5464
(800) 922–5651 (SC residents)

Branch office:
ACS Fort Jackson (803) 751–
5256
William Meares, Counselor

Family Service Greenville
Consumer Credit
Counseling Division
PO Box 10306, Federal
Station
Greenville, SC 29603
David C. Shiel, ACSW,
Executive Director
Willisteen Talbert, Program
Director
(803) 232–2434, 232–6266

South Dakota

Consumer Credit Counseling
Service of the Black Hills
517 Main Street
PO Box 14
Rapid City, SD 57709
Diane Trithart, Executive
Director
(605) 348–4550

Branch office:
Gillette, WY (307) 686–1939

Satellite office:
Ellsworth Air Force Base
(605) 385–4663

Lutheran Social Services of
South Dakota
CCCS Division
617 West 11th Street
Sioux Falls, SD 57104
Judy Reinke, Program
Director
(605) 336–2005

Satellite office:
Watertown (605) 882–2740

Tennessee

Family & Children's Services
of Chattanooga
CCCS Division
300 East 8th Street
Chattanooga, TN 37402
Tommy Perkins, Executive
Director
(615) 755–2860

Satellite office:
Dalton, GA (404) 226–4357

Consumer Credit Counseling
Service of Greater
Knoxville, Inc.
1012 Heiskell Avenue
PO Box 3924
Knoxville, TN 37927–3924
Sue L. Brown, President and
CEO
(615) 522–2661, 522–7151

Satellite offices:
Morristown
Oak Ridge
(Schedule appointments
through Knoxville office)
(615) 522–2661

Consumer Credit Counseling
Service
(A division of Family Service
of Memphis)
2400 Poplar Avenue, Suite
500
Memphis, TN 38112
Abbott L. Jordan, Executive
Director
Lucinda Nance, Program
Director, CCCS
(901) 323–4909

Consumer Credit Counseling
Service of Metropolitan
Nashville, Inc.
250 Venture Circle, Suite 205
Nashville, TN 37228–1604
Marvin N. Wright, Executive
Director
(615) 244–5184, 244–5185

Texas

Child and Family Service,
Inc. Consumer Credit
Counseling Division
1221 West Ben White
Boulevard, Suite 112 B
Austin, TX 78704
Lonnie Williams, CCCS
Director
(512) 447–0711

Satellite offices:
Bergstrom Air Force Base
Round Rock
(Schedule appointments
through Austin office)
(512) 447–0711

Consumer Credit Counseling
Center of South Texas
1721 South Brownlee
Boulevard
Corpus Christi, TX 78404
David C. Melton, President
Rosemary Cretin, Services
Supervisor
(512) 882–1791

Branch office:
Rio Grande Valley (800) 333–
HELP

Satellite office:
Kingsville Naval Air Station

(Schedule appointments
through Corpus Christi
office)
(512) 882–1791

Consumer Credit Counseling
Service of Greater Dallas,
Inc.
1949 Stemmons Freeway,
Suite 200
Dallas, TX 75207
David H. Dugan, President
(214) 748–CCCS

Branch offices:
Amarillo (806) 358–2221
Arlington (817) 633–4357
Carrollton (214) 242–6548
Duncanville (214) 709–3000
Mesquite (214) 216–0488
Richardson (214) 437–6252
Wichita Falls (817) 696–2227

Consumer Credit Counseling
Service
YWCA
1600 North Brown Street
El Paso, TX 79902
Darlene Gade, Executive
Director
(915) 533–7475

Consumer Credit Counseling
Service of Greater Fort
Worth, Inc.
807 Texas Street, Suite 100
Fort Worth, TX 76102
Warren E. Coggins, President
(817) 334–0151
(800) 541–2227
(800) 541–CCCS toll free

Branch offices:
Lubbock (806) 784–1041
Waco (817) 772–0007

Satellite office:
Temple (817) 772–0007

Consumer Credit Counseling Service of Houston and the Gulf Coast Area, Inc.
4203 Fannin Street
Houston, TX 77004
Terry M. Blaney, President
(713) 520–0742

Branch offices:
Bay Area (713) 520–0742
Baytown (713) 520–0742
Beaumont (409) 721–9511
Brazosport (800) 338–8622
Bryan/College Station (409) 822–6110
Fort Bend County (713) 520–0742
Galveston (800) 338–8622
Montgomery County (713) 520–0742
Pasadena (713) 520–0742
West Houston (713) 520–0742

(Schedule appointments through Houston office)
(713) 520–0742 (residents of area code 713)
(800) 338–8622 (residents outside area code 713)

Consumer Credit Counseling of North Central Texas, Inc.
1006 West University Drive
McKinney, TX 75069
Pamela Gray, Executive Director
(214) 542–0257

Branch office:
Plano (214) 964–2022

Satellite offices:
Denton (817) 382–0331
Greenville (214) 455–3987
Sherman (214) 892–6927

Consumer Credit Counseling Service of Greater San Antonio, Inc.
4203 Woodcock, Suite 251
San Antonio, TX 78228
Ruby Bainum, Executive Director
(512) 734–8112

Branch office:
San Antonio (512) 657–6007

Utah

Community Consumer Credit Counseling Service of Northern Utah, Inc.
2751 Washington Boulevard, Upper Level
Ogden, UT 84402
Brent Littlefield, President
(801) 394–7759

Consumer Credit Counseling Service of Utah, Inc.
845 East 4800 South, Suite 200
Murray, UT 84107
Dale G. Taylor, Executive Director
(801) 266–0064

Vermont

Consumer Credit Counseling
Service of New Hampshire
and Vermont
(Branch of CCCS, Concord,
NH)
Bennington
Brattleboro
Rutland

(Schedule appointments
through Concord, NH
office)
(800) 327–6778

Virginia

Consumer Credit Counseling
Service of Alexandria
(Branch of CCCS of Greater
Washington)
801 North Pitt Street, Suite
101
Alexandria, VA 22314
Marilyn Morgan, Branch
Director
(703) 836–8772

Consumer Credit Counseling
Service of Northern
Virginia
(Branch of CCCS of Greater
Washington)
10400 Eaton Place, Suite
102A
Fairfax, VA 22030

Judy McCoid, Branch
Director
(703) 591–9020

Peninsula Family Service,
Inc.
CCCS Division
1520 Aberdeen Road
PO Box 7315
Hampton, VA 23666
Faye C. Webb, President and
CEO
(804) 827–8344

Satellite office:
Williamsburg (804) 874–6580

Consumer Credit Counseling
Service of Central Virginia
1010 Miller Park Square
Lynchburg, VA 24501
Nancy K. Young, Executive
Director
(804) 847–4447

Consumer Credit Counseling
Service of Prince William
County
(Branch of CCCS of Greater
Washington)
8088 Sudley Road, Suite F
Manassas, VA 22110
Laura Fye, Counselor
(703) 690–4779

Consumer Credit Counseling
Service of Tidewater
(Division of Family Services)
222 West 19th Street
Norfolk, VA 23517
Doris L. Eskey, Program
Coordinator
(804) 622–7017

Branch office:
Virginia Beach—Lynnhaven
Road

(Schedule appointments
through Norfolk office)
(804) 622–7017

Satellite offices:
Chesapeake
Franklin
Suffolk
Virginia Beach—South
Boulevard

(Schedule appointments
through Norfolk office)
(804) 622–7017

Consumer Credit Counseling
Service of Virginia, Inc.
6 North Sixth Street, Suite
200
Richmond, VA 23219
Robert E. Bryan, Executive
Director
(804) 780–9042

Branch offices:
Charlottesville (804) 977–
9596

Colonial Heights (804) 520–
8744
Fredericksburg (703) 371–
7575
Virginia Beach (804) 424–
2060

Consumer Credit Counseling
Services of Roanoke Valley,
Inc.
3102 B. Peters Creek Road,
NW
Roanoke, VA 24019
Virginia H. Gayle, Executive
Director
(703) 563–0076

Washington

Consumer Credit Counseling
Service of the Tri-Cities
11 South Cascade
PO Box 6551
Kennewick, WA 99336
Thelma Flanagan, Executive
Director
(509) 586–2181

Consumer Credit Counseling
Service of Seattle
2326 Sixth Avenue, Suite 206
Seattle, WA 98121
Chuck Schutzman, President
(206) 441–3291

Branch offices:
Everett (206) 441–3291
Mt. Vernon (206) 257–8053

Oak Harbor (206) 257–8053
Whidby Island/Naval Air
Station (206) 257–8053

Consumer Credit Counseling
Service of the Inland
Empire
West 521 Maxwell
PO Box 5393
Spokane, WA 99205
Lori Gregg, Executive
Director
(509) 455–5568

Consumer Credit Counseling
Service of Tacoma-Pierce
County
11306 Bridgeport Way, SW
Tacoma, WA 98499
Laura G. Johnson, Executive
Director
(206) 588–1858

Satellite offices:
McChord Air Force Base,
McChord (206) 588–1858
Naval Submarine Base,
Bangor (206) 396–4115
Puget Sound Naval Shipyard
(206) 476–5113
United Way of Kitsap County
(206) 373–2182

Consumer Credit Counseling
Service of Yakima Valley
307 North 3rd Street, Suite 2
PO Box 511
Yakima, WA 98901
Georgia W. Norcott,
Executive Director
(509) 248–5270

Satellite office:
Wenatchee (509) 662–2116

West Virginia

Consumer Credit Counseling
Service of Southern West
Virginia, Inc.
PO Box 2129
Beckley, WV 25802
Raymond Coleman,
Executive Director
(304) 255–2499

Consumer Credit Counseling
Service of the Kanawha
Valley
8 Capitol Street
503 Terminal Building
Charleston, WV 25301
Geraldine Allen, Manager
(304) 344–3843

Consumer Credit Counseling
Service of North Central
West Virginia
Criss-Cross, Inc.
166 Washington Avenue
PO Box 1831
Clarksburg, WV 26301
Edward Welp, MSW
Executive Director
Marie Battles, Manager
(304) 623–0921

Satellite office:
Morgantown (304) 291–6819

Consumer Credit Counseling
of Family Service, Inc.
1304 Fifth Avenue
Huntington, WV 25701
Barbara Tinsman, Executive
Director
(304) 522–4321

Consumer Credit Counseling
Service of the Mid-Ohio
Valley, Inc.
2715 Murdoch Avenue, B-4
Beechwood Plaza
Parkersburg, WV 26101
June Shelene, Manager
(304) 485–3141, 485–6280

Family Service—Upper Ohio
Valley CCCS of the Upper
Ohio Valley
51 11th Street
Wheeling, WV 26003
Lonnie Wineman, Executive
Vice President
Shelly Meadows, CCCS
Director
(304) 232–6733

Satellite office:
Steubenville, OH
(614) 283–4763

Wisconsin

no service

Wyoming

Gillette (307) 686–1939
(Branch office of Rapid City,
SD)
Southern Wyoming, refer to
Fort Collins, CO
(303) 484–7520

Canadian Agencies Affiliated with the National Foundation for Consumer Credit

Credit Counselling Service of Metroplitan Toronto
100 Lombard Street, Suite 301
Toronto, Ontario M5C 1M3

Beulah ("Sam") Hastings, Executive Director
(416) 366–5251

Branch office:
Scarborough (416) 757–8316

For further information on Canadian counseling locations contact:

The Ontario Association of Credit Counselling Services
72A Main Street West
Grimsby, Ontario L3M 1R6

Mailing Address:
PO Box 189
Grimsby, Ontario L3M 4G5
Susan Juhlke-Ongaro, Executive Director
(416) 945–5644

New service:
Ontario Credit Counselling Access
Box 278
Grimsby, Ontario L3M 4G5
(800) 263–0260

Index

About the Author

William Kent Brunette has helped hundreds of people free themselves of debt and credit-related problems. He regularly conducts "Financial Responsibility" seminars for alcoholism and substance-abuse clinics throughout the United States. According to many patients and clinic staffs, these presentations have become one of the most popular and beneficial components of the clinics' programs.

Mr. Brunette has also provided individual counseling to countless others whose financial problems required special attention. As an attorney and member of the District of Columbia and Texas bars, he has represented numerous clients in credit-related matters. Many of these efforts involved resolving disputes with creditors and clearing up adverse credit reports.

As the chief lobbyist on financial service issues for the American Association of Retired Persons (AARP), Mr. Brunette is intimately familiar with all the consumer credit statutes. Through his daily interaction with congressional committees, federal regulatory banking and enforcement agencies, and executive departments, he is aware of and has an influence on the latest financial service developments.

Mr. Brunette, who lives in Washington, D.C., has also researched extensively the range of consumer credit and personal finance issues confronting those experiencing credit difficulty.